LETTERS TO THE HON'BLE PRIME MINISTER

PART X

THE BOOK IS A THINK TANK, COMPRISING INNOVATIVE AND ORIGINAL CONCEPTS BY THE AUTHOR, AN ORIGINAL THINKER, OFFERING SUGGESTIONS FOR MAKING BHARAT A DEVELOPED COUNTRY AND ACHIEVING GLOBAL PEACE.

Dr. Nanda Nandan Das

NOTION PRESS

NOTION PRESS

India. Singapore. Malaysia.

Author:

DR. Nanda Nandan Das, Original Thinker
D. Sc, D. Litt, PDF (South Korea), PhD (Road), PhD (Building),
M.S.W, B.Sc. (Engg.), LLB, F.I.E, M.I.R.C, M.I.B.C
Former Secretary, Works, Government of Odisha
Former Chairman, O.B & C.C
Chairman, People's Welfare Suggestion Forum
Ex-Chairman, Odisha Durneeti Sangharsa Mancha
Ex-Team Leader, Mott. Mac Donald
Ex-Consultant, POSCO-INDIA
Address:
Plot. No. 2024, Chintamaniswar Area, Bhubaneswar-751006,
Odisha, India Mob. +91-9437617604
E-mail: nandanandan_das@yahoo.com

COUNTRIES VISITED- USA, CANADA, BRITAIN, GERMANY, FRANCE, SWITZERLAND, LIECHTENSTEIN, NETHERLAND, BELGIUM, ITALY, AUSTRIA, VATICAN, DUBAI, ABU DHABI, SOUTH AFRICA, AUSTRALIA, NEW ZEALAND, FIJI, CHINA, JAPAN, THAILAND, MALAYSIA, SINGAPORE, NEPAL AND SRI LANKA.

Editor:
Er. Shree Nandan Das

Chief Editor:
Prof. Purnima Mitra
First Edition: 2024

Dedicated to
Entire Global Family to live in PEACE in
Esteemed Mother Earth

CONTENTS

THE AUTHOR'S VIEW

The contents of this book are a compilation of my suggestions to the Hon'ble Prime Minister of India, focusing on various strategies for the nation's development. I firmly believe that all humanity is one family, united under the care of Mother Earth, irrespective of nationality or identity. As inhabitants of this shared planet, it is our collective duty to strive for harmony and well-being. My contributions to the United Nations reflect my unwavering commitment to achieving global peace.

Every concept presented in this book is original, born from spontaneous moments of inspiration, often at the most unusual hours. These ideas were later developed into articles and, following rigorous discussions with experts, were shared with the Hon'ble Prime Minister and other relevant authorities. My work is also documented in twelve volumes titled Letters to the Hon'ble Prime Minister, which are available online. These volumes address critical challenges facing the country and propose pathways to global harmony. I am confident that if any developing or underdeveloped nation adopts these principles with sincerity, they will experience significant progress.

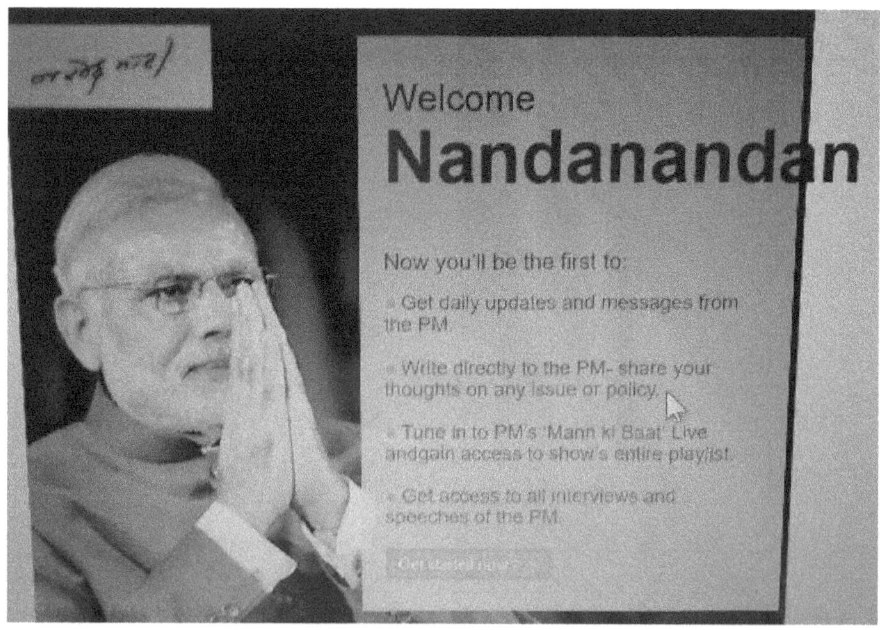

One of the defining moments in my journey was the warm reception I received from the Hon'ble Prime Minister of Bharat, Shri Narendra Modi Ji, in 2019. It fills me with immense satisfaction to see many of my ideas reflected in his speeches at the United Nations and in the Indian Parliament.

One cherished memory is a letter I received from the Hon'ble Prime Minister dated October 4, 2024. It stands as a source of immense pride not only for me but also for my family and community. The Hon'ble Prime Minister's words, "Your trust, support, and cooperation are my real treasure. Your affectionate words fill me with new energy to strive in service of the nation. In the third term of our government, my resolve to fulfil the aspirations of the people and take India to great heights of progress has further strengthened," left me overwhelmed and deeply moved. I feel profound gratitude for such an encouraging acknowledgment.

This journey of contributing to the nation's growth and vision has been both humbling and fulfilling. I hope my work continues to inspire progress, unity, and peace for all.

Beyond these contributions, I have also made discoveries related to fundamental aspects of Earth sciences, including the Earth's rotation on its axis in an anti-clockwise direction (resulting in day and night), the Moon's revolution around the Earth over a month, and the existence of the Earth's magnetic field. These findings were communicated to ISRO and the Hon'ble Prime Minister as evidence of my dedication to advancing knowledge.

Dr. Nanda Nandan Das, Original Thinker,
The Author

EDITORIAL DESK

Dr. Nanda Nandan Das, born on December 21, 1943, in the village of Baudpur, Bhadrak, Odisha, Bharat, is a distinguished figure in the realm of engineering and administrative services. He embarked on his professional journey diligently after obtaining a BSc (Engg) from UCE, Burla, in 1965. His illustrious career culminated in a more sharpened manner when he got retired as the Secretary of Works Govt. of Odisha and Chairman of O.B & C.C. on December 31, 2001. His unwavering dedication towards his duty and innovative problem-solving abilities made him a trailblazer, consistently demonstrating that nothing is insurmountable.

Recognition and accolades have followed Dr. Nanda Nandan Das throughout his career:

State Awards: Six prestigious honours from "The Institution of Engineers India, Odisha Centre, Bhubaneswar" in 2002, 2003, 2004, 2006, 2016, and 2017.

National Recognition: Rashtriya Gourav Award - Certificate of Excellence presented by Dr. G.V.G. Krishnamurty, the Honourable Former Election Commissioner, in 2004.

International Acknowledgment: PDF, South Korea, recognized Dr. Nanda Nandan Das's contributions in 2016.

- Gopabandhu Das Samman in 2019
- Madhusudan Das Samman in 2020.
- Original Thinker Award in 2018.
- Lifetime Achievement Award from 'The Institution of Engineers India, Odisha Centre' in 2013.
- Felicitation by ISTE, Odisha Section, in 2017.

Dr. Nanda Nandan Das's remarkable achievements extend beyond his professional life.

- Being a confident swimmer, he saves four lives from perilous situations in rivers like the Ganges, Salandi, and Indravati.
- His globetrotting experiences have taken him to numerous countries.
- In the realm of scientific discovery, Dr. Nanda Nandan Das stands as a pioneer.
    i. He proposed a ground breaking theory on the Earth's rotation on its axis, resulting in day and night, as well as

the Moon's revolution around the Earth, leading to the concept of a month.

ii. His innovative concept of the existence of a magnetic field in Earth due to the rotation of Earth on its axis, a thought-provoking mystery, has been sent to ISRO and Hon'ble Prime Minister, India. These discoveries have been referred to ISRO and Hon'ble Prime Minister, India

Dr. Nanda Nandan Das's literary contributions are equally noteworthy, with 18 published books to his name. Notable works include "Letters to the Hon'ble Prime Minister Part IA, Part IB, Part IC, Part II, Part III, Part IV, Part V, Part VI, Part VII, Part VIII, Part IX, & Part X "(twelve Volumes available online.), which delves into administrative reforms in Bharat. If any developing/under-developed country would follow these innovative concepts sincerely, then it would be developed soon. His book 'Global Peace', was sent to the Presidents/ Prime Ministers of about 170 countries during 2017. This effort led to significant diplomatic developments, including the meeting between the Presidents of America and North Korea in Singapore on June 12, 2018, on 'Global Peace' (available online).

Dr. Nanda Nandan Das's devotion to social causes is also evident. He proposed the implementation of the Indian Citizenship Card to the Ministry of Home Affairs in 2009, a concept that later evolved into the Aadhaar Card. Keeping him isolated with undisturbed mind, he tirelessly suggests innovative ideas to the Honourable Prime Minister of Bharat to create a crime and poverty free nation. Additionally, he advocates for the inclusion of Moral Science, (Already suggested the course from class 1 to graduation, based on all being Indians and how to make the country developed) in educational curriculum for the reformation of the country.

Dr. Nanda Nandan Das's ultimate aim is to foster patriotism, ingenuity, quality, and moral values among citizens, both in Bharat and globally. He envisions a world where countries function as a united family, and "Religion Humanity" takes precedence over any religious divide.

Throughout his tenure, Dr. Nanda Nandan Das initiated successful projects, such as installing statues of deities in government buildings to prevent spitting on the walls, hindering unhygienic and disrespectful attitudes. His dedication to service has been recognized by the national daily, The Hindustan Times, during 2002, among others.

His entry in Universe, Earth, Country, State, District, Village:

1.   The Universe: - Rotation of Earth on its axis forming day & night, existence of magnetic field on Earth, the causes still remain a mystery, but have been discovered by Dr. Das.

2.   The Earth: His book GLOBAL PEACE had been sent to heads of 170 countries achieving peace globally.

3.   The Country: He initiated to introduce Indian ID card during 2009, and the outcome is the Aadhaar Card. Due to the inspiration of PM, Dr. Das suggested many issues, which are included in 12 books of 'Letters to the Hon'ble Prime Minister', available-Amazon and Flipchart.

4.   The State: The OVERDRAFT of the state has been stopped due to his suggestion to the finance minister during 2005. Best Engineer of the state, is being awarded 'Dr. Nanda Nandan Das Award' every year by Institution of Engineers, India, Bhubaneswar.

5.   The district: -He developed roads, constructed new Rajghat Bridge, renovated some high schools.

6.   The Village: He developed road, school, and Pravat Club.

This book 'Letters to the Hon'ble Prime Minister' is a reservoir of instant solutions and a comprehensive encyclopaedia dedicated to our beloved Motherland, Bharat.

Prof. Purnima Mitra,
The Chief Editor,
Asst. Professor,
NIIS Group of Institution

CHAPTER I

A BEACON OF SUPPORT: SHRI NARENDRA MODI JI, HON'BLE PM'S TRIBUTE TO NANDA NANDAN DAS

The letter from Shri Narendra Modi Ji, Hon'ble Prime Minister of India, to Nanda Nandan Das conveys the heartfelt message: *"Your trust, support, and cooperation are my real treasures. Your affectionate words fill me with renewed energy to strive in service of the nation. In the third term of our government, my resolve to fulfil the aspirations of the people and elevate India to new heights of progress has grown even stronger."* These words from Shri Narendra Modi Ji are deeply inspiring and evoke a sense of profound gratitude.

Shri Nanda Nandan Das Ji,

Heartfelt gratitude to you for sending warm birthday wishes. I am overwhelmed to receive greetings from my family members such as yourself from across the country.

Your trust, support and cooperation are my real treasure. Your affectionate words fill me with new energy to strive in service of the nation. In the third term of our government, my resolve to fulfil the aspirations of the people and take India to great heights of progress has further strengthened.

Powered by the ability of our people and the skills of our youth, we have been setting new benchmarks in development over the last 10 years. *Amrit Kaal* is an opportunity to scale up our efforts to build a developed, inclusive and self-reliant nation.

The contribution of every Indian towards the progress of the nation is deeply valued.

With best wishes for your good health, happiness and prosperity.

Yours,

(Narendra Modi)

Shri Nanda Nandan Das
Plot- 2024, Chintamaniswar Area
Bhubaneswar, District- Khordha
Odisha- 751006

They reflect recognition of Nanda Nandan Das sincere efforts for the welfare of the people, nation, and peace on Planet Earth. This acknowledgment motivates him to continue striving with greater dedication and pride.

CHAPTER II

WORLD LEADERS AND THE UNITED NATIONS MUST INTERVENE TO END WAR AND PROMOTE PEACE

Registration Number: PMOPG/E/2024/0174890

Dt. **03.12.2024**

Respected Shri Narendra Modi Ji, Hon'ble Prime Minister of India,

I wish to bring to your esteemed attention a significant virtual assembly the 107th session of the Thinkers' Club held on 1st December 2024 via the Zoom platform. The session focused on the urgent and intricate topic of "War and Peace" in the current global context.

The detailed deliberations and recommendations from this session are enclosed herewith for your kind consideration and appropriate action.

With warm regards and sincere hope for a peaceful world,
Yours faithfully,
Nanda Nandan Das, Original Thinker
Chairman, People's Welfare Suggestion Forum
03.12.2024

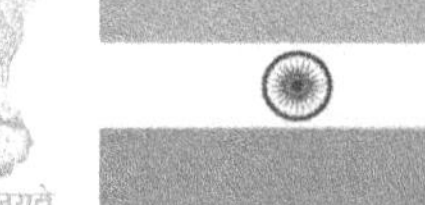

NARENDRA MODI, PRIME MINISTER

Name Of Complainant-NANDA NANDAN DAS
Date of Receipt-03/12/2024
Received By Ministry/Department-Prime Minister's Office

WORLD LEADERS AND UN SHOULD INTERFERE TO STOP WAR & ESTABLISH PEACE

3rd December 2024 Bhubaneswar, Odisha -
In a significant virtual gathering, the 107th session of the Thinkers' Club, held over the Zoom platform, delved into the complex and tumultuous global landscape of "War and Peace" on 1st December 2024.

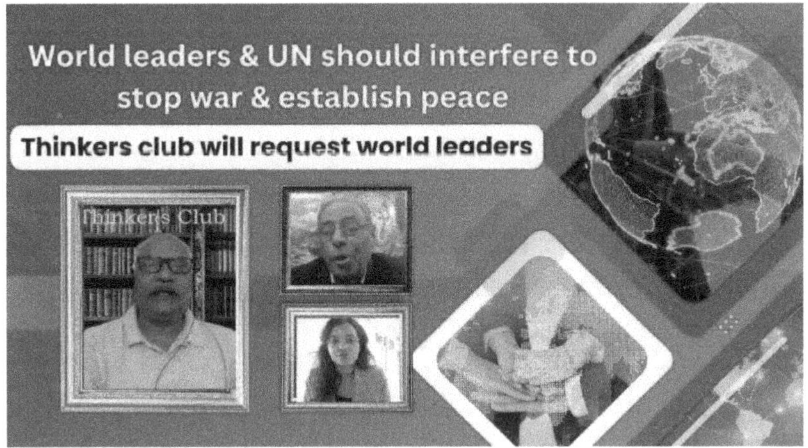

Key Speakers and Participants
The session was presided over by Dr. Nanda Nandan Das, a retired former Works Secretary of the Government of Odisha. Sri Vivek Pattanayak, a retired IAS officer, served as the Chief Guest. Retired Major General Atanu Pattanaik was the chief speaker, providing insightful perspectives on global conflicts. Sri Barada Das, President of the Thinkers' Club, moderated the discussion with precision and depth.

Historical Context and Current Challenges
The discussion highlighted that since World War II ended in 1945 with twice nuclear bombings on 6th & 9th August 1945 in Hiroshima & Nagasaki of Japan. To maintain peace and security

internationally on Earth United Nation (UN) was created on 24th October 1945. Several major conflicts have continued to disrupt global peace. These include:

Korean War: A conflict that began in 1950 and remains unresolved.

Vietnam War: A prolonged conflict from 1955 to 1975.

Gulf War: Initiated in 1990 following Iraq's invasion of Kuwait.

Ukraine War: Ongoing tensions between Ukraine and Russia.

Israel-Palestine Conflicts: Decades-long disputes over territory and sovereignty.

The establishment of the League of Nations after World War I failed to prevent subsequent wars; similarly, today's United Nations Organization (UNO) faces significant challenges in maintaining global peace due to veto powers held by five major countries.

Economic Interests and Lobbying

According to Major General Atanu Pattanaik, economic interests are at the core of most wars. He emphasized that lobbies such as those representing:

Pharmaceuticals: Influencing health policies for profit.

Petroleum: Resisting transitions to renewable energy sources.

Weapons Manufacturing: Benefiting from ongoing conflicts.

Additional factors include ego-driven supremacy battles and ethnic tensions. Pattanaik noted that leaders prioritize their own interests over global peace and that industries like weapons manufacturing benefit from ongoing wars.

Critique of Global Leadership

The meeting underscored a lack of genuine leadership on the global stage. Leaders are seen as more concerned with their own agendas than with fostering world peace. The war industry's billion-dollar market and lobbying efforts by pharmaceutical and petroleum industries were cited as examples where profit overrides public health and environmental concerns.

Dr. Nanda Nandan Das has outlined a vision for achieving global peace. His suggestions, conveyed to the Hon'ble Prime Minister of Bharat on 6th November 2024 under registration number PMOPG/E/2024/0163312, and later to the United Nations Security Council on 23rd November 2024, emphasize a unified approach toward harmony among nations.

Here are the key points from Dr. Das's proposal on way to achieve Global peace:

Narrator (continued): The discussion begins with an exploration of the origins of humanity. Earth, separated from the Sun approximately 4.5 billion years ago, cooled over millennia, forming water and enabling life. Early humans, believed to have originated in Africa over 100,000 years ago, spread across the globe, forming civilizations, languages, religions, races, and nations. Unfortunately, these divisions, combined with egotism, religious differences, expansion mind-set and the pursuit of power, have fuelled conflicts throughout history. All are one family of Mother Earth and one's existence finite like other living beings. Nothing belongs one even own body, soul or breath.

To counter this cycle, Dr. Das proposes a path to global peace:

1. **Global Unity:** Recognize all human beings as part of one global family sharing Planet Earth.
2. **Finite Life, Infinite Harmony:** Work collectively to promote peace and harmony, benefiting all humanity.
3. **Freedom of Faith:** Religion is a personal and social bond. Everyone should practice their beliefs without imposing on others.
4. **Leadership Accountability:** National leaders must prioritize the welfare and development of their citizens while acting as representatives within the United Nations framework.
5. **Global Defence Regulation:** The United Nations should oversee global defence systems to prevent conflicts and wars.
6. **Nuclear Energy for Good:** Nuclear energy must be harnessed solely for space exploration, disaster management, and humanitarian welfare.

7. **Democratic Decision-Making:** International resolutions should reflect the majority opinion during discussions.
8. **Value-Based Education:** Education systems worldwide should incorporate a curriculum promoting the idea of one human race, transcending cultural, religious, and geographical differences. Dr. Das's book, Moral Science, which outlines these values, has been shared with leaders from 170 nations.
9. **Eradicating Terrorism:** All forms of terrorism must be condemned and dealt with severely.
10. **Universal Concepts (Copyrighted by Dr. N.N. Das):**
    o **Gods:** The Sun, Earth, and one's parents, as they sustain life.
    o **Religion:** Humanity is the true religion; all people belong to one race.
    o **Caste:** There are only two natural distinctions—male and female—with equal rights for all.

Participants expressed a dire need for revitalizing institutions like UNO and G20 to address these issues effectively. It was decided that letters would be sent by the Thinkers' Club to the UN Security Council and other stakeholders expressing their concerns.

International Participation

Sri Vivek Pattanayak IAS, Dr. Nanda Nandan Das, a retired former Works Secretary of the Government of Odisha. Retired Major General, Atanu Pattanaik a retired IAS officer Dr. Bhagya Sree Singh from London delivered the welcome speech, setting the tone for a comprehensive discussion. Other participants included Jayakrushna Choudhury, Binod Das, Pratap Rout, and Dipayan Pattanaik. The meeting drew participation from numerous intellectuals both directly on Zoom and through YouTube.

Conclusion

These principles aim to unify humanity and lay the foundation for a peaceful, inclusive world. We encourage a comprehensive review of these suggestions to make strides toward global harmony. This gathering underscore a pressing need for renewed commitment to global peace initiatives a midst ongoing geopolitical tensions and economic lobbying influences. World leaders, UN should interfere to stop war & establish peace. As Global Citizens, it is imperative to demand more from our leaders and international institutions to ensure a more peaceful and equitable world.

Barada Prasanna Das

President Thinker Club

03.12.2024

Current Status-Case closed

Date of Action-15/12/2024

Remarks: Your suggestions are always welcome. Should you have any other suggestions Register on MyGov App. You can Follow MyGov on Twitter/Subscribe to MyGov YouTube Channel also. Regards, CPIO MyGov

Rating-Excellent

Rating Remarks-Satisfied

Officer Name-Office of CEO MyGov (Office of CEO MyGov)

Organisation name-My Gov.

Contact Address-Electronics Niketan CGO Complex, New Delhi

Email Address-ceo@mygov.in

Contact Number-01124364706

CHAPTER III

BHARAT AS HINDU RASTRA

Registration Number: PMOPG/E/2024/0152321

Dt. 10.10.2024

Respected Shri Narendra Modi Ji, Hon'ble Prime Minister, India,

I hope this letter finds you in good health and high spirits. Recently, I came across disturbing news on television regarding an Islamic preacher from Bangladesh who made a public announcement with the intent to convert Bharat into a Muslim nation. This call, along with hostile actions and threats towards Hindus, is deeply concerning. It is crucial to reflect on the ongoing efforts by certain groups, supported by external forces like Pakistan, to undermine the integrity of our country and impose their ideologies, often through intimidation and violence.

At the time of India's independence, a separate nation, Pakistan, was created to accommodate Muslims, which later split into Pakistan and Bangladesh. If certain groups within the Muslim community feel discontent living in Bharat, they have the option to seek refuge in these nations.

In light of these developments, I humbly request that the Government of India bring international attention to the alarming activities of extremist elements, both within and outside our country. It is imperative to take firm and decisive action. Considering the ancient heritage of Hindu culture and the principles of "Vasudhaiva Kutumbakam" (the world is one family) and "Sarve Bhavantu Sukhinah" (may all beings be happy), I urge you to consider declaring Bharat a Hindu Rashtra.

This, however, should not be exclusionary. It should promote peaceful coexistence for all communities, including Muslims, based on the values of Sanatan Dharma, ensuring that the safety, dignity, and cultural rights of Hindus are preserved. I appeal to you to take measures to protect Hindus before it is too late.

Thank you for your attention to this grave matter.

Yours sincerely,

Dr. Nanda Nandan Das, Original Thinker

Chairman, People's Welfare Suggestion Forum

Dt. 10.10.2024   Time 5;30 pm

Name Of Complainant-NANDA NANDAN DAS

Date of Receipt-10/10/2024

Current Status-Case closed

Date of Action-11/10/2024

Remarks-GEN. COMMENTS NOT CONTAINING SPECIFIC GRIEVANCE

Officer Name-Mukul Dixit (Under Secretary (Public))

Organisation name-Prime Minister's Office

Address-Public Wing 5th Floor, Rail Bhawan New Delhi

My write up on receiving the remark 'Current Status-Case closed, Date of Action-11/10/2024

Remarks-GEN. COMMENTS NOT CONTAINING SPECIFIC GRIEVANCE' as above is furnished to Hon'ble Prime Minister. The details are followed:

Your grievance has been registered successfully-. Registration No.: PMOPG/E/2024/0156301

Dt. 20.10.2024   5:30 am

BHARAT AS HINDU RASTRA

Respected Shri Narendra Modi Ji, Hon'ble Prime Minister of India, I have been sharing my innovative thoughts and suggestions with your esteemed office since 2019, after receiving an encouraging message from your side (attached herewith). In that message, you welcomed me with these words:

- "Welcome, Nandanandan. Now you'll be the first to:

- Get daily updates and messages from the PM.

- Write directly to the PM and share your thoughts on any issue or policy.

- Tune in to PM's 'Mann ki Baat' live and access the entire playlist of the show.

- Access all interviews and speeches of the PM. Get started now."

This message opened a link, allowing me to share my thoughts with you directly. Since then, I have regularly communicated my suggestions with your office. An icon was also created on my mobile phone, which allowed me to receive daily updates and messages from you, Hon'ble PM. I have been receiving proper responses to my suggestions over the years, and it filled me with great satisfaction to see some of my ideas coincidentally reflected in your speeches at the UNGA, in Parliament, and in public meetings.

All my write-ups, which address various issues and propose solutions, are intended for your direct knowledge, Hon'ble Prime Minister. My suggestions were usually forwarded to the PMO, and the concerned contact officer, Shri Ambuj Sharma (then Under Secretary, Public), along with other authorities at the Prime Minister's Office, would respond. However, as the officers have since been transferred, the current authorities may not be fully aware of the previous communication. They seem to view my innovative suggestions as mere grievances and provide remarks based on their own perspectives without delving deeply into the solutions proposed. I am an 80+ year-old man, living in isolation in my native village, Baudpur, Bhadrak District, away from my family. Despite my age, my mind continues to work effectively, and I often find myself spontaneously developing solutions to major and critical issues facing our country, particularly during the night, between 10 p.m. and 3 a.m. I always make it a point to jot down these thoughts immediately, as they do not return once missed.

Currently, the system for submitting suggestions seems to have changed, and I am not supported by any IT professional. As a result, I have resorted to using the 'Public Grievance' system to send my innovative thoughts, though they are not grievances but solutions meant for your direct attention. I fear that my suggestions may no longer be reaching you. To clarify, I have attached the original message from your office in PDF attached-format. Therefore, I humbly request that you kindly review the attached file, which contains my suggestions along with the final remarks from the PMO. If the current method of submission through the

LETTERS TO THE HON'BLE PRIME MINISTER, PART- X

'Public Grievance' system is not appropriate for these types of ideas, I request that you kindly provide an alternative link with contact details of the responsible officers. I also ask that my innovative thoughts be thoroughly reviewed by experts with a research-oriented mindset. With my heartfelt regards, Yours sincerely,

Dr. Nanda Nandan Das, Original Thinker Former Secretary, Govt. of Odisha Chairman, People's Welfare Suggestion Forum.

Dt. 20.10.2024

NARENDRA MODI

Prime Minister of India

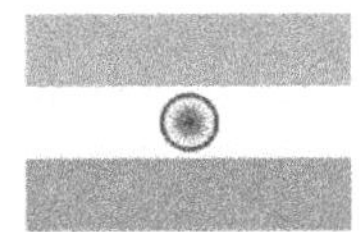

Date of Receipt-20/10/2024

Received By Ministry/Department -Prime Minister's Office

Current Status-Case closed

Date of Action-02/11/2024

Remarks: Your suggestions are always welcome. Should you have any other suggestions Register on MyGov App. You can Follow MyGov on Twitter/Subscribe to MyGov YouTube Channel also.

Rating ☆☆☆☆☆ Very Good

Rating Remarks Satisfied

Regards, CPIO MyGov

Rating Remarks-Satisfied

Officer Name-Office of CEO MyGov (Office of CEO MyGov).

Contact Address-Electronics Niketan CGO Complex, New Delhi

Email Address-ceo@mygov.in

Contact Number-01124364706

CHAPTER IV

OFFICER ASSIGNED TO REVIEW TO BE HONEST AND RESEARCH MIND-SET

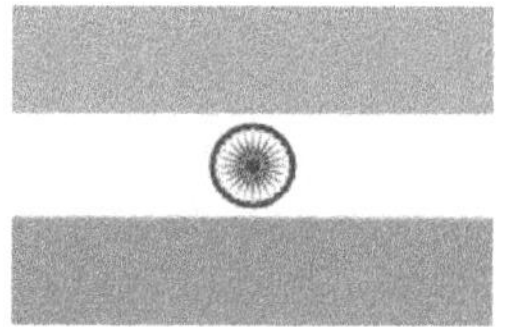

NARENDRA MODI
Prime Minister of India

Name Of Complainant-NANDA NANDAN DAS
Date of Receipt-15/10/2024
Received By Ministry/Department-Prime Minister's Office
Grievance Description Respected Shri Narendra Modi Ji, Hon'ble Prime Minister of India, On 14th October 2024, I received two calls from the Prime Minister's Office (PMO) regarding the closure of cases associated with the registration numbers PMOPG/E/2024/0150147 (dated 5th October 2024) and PMOPG/E/2024/0151005 (dated 8th October 2024). I would like to respectfully clarify that my submissions to the Hon'ble Prime Minister are original thoughts and suggestions, not grievances. The submission under PMOPG/E/2024/0150147, which presents a solution to issues related to PoK, has been resubmitted under

registration number PMOPG/E/2024/0153901 on 15th October 2024.

I was informed by phone from the PMO that the case linked to registration number PMOPG/E/2024/0151005 (dated 8th October 2024) has been closed with the following details: Date of Action: 9th October 2024 Remarks: General comments not containing specific grievance Rating: Poor Rating Remarks: Not Satisfied Officer Name: Shri Mukul Dixit (Under Secretary, Public) Organization: Prime Minister's Office It seems that my suggestions, which are based on original and carefully considered thoughts, may not have been given the attention they deserve. These proposals touch upon critical issues concerning the future safety and well-being of the nation. My thoughts often come to me during odd hours, and at the time of writing this letter, it is 2:05 AM on 15th October 2024. I have resubmitted my proposal for your kind consideration. I humbly request that the officer assigned to review it be one with an honest and research-oriented mind-set, as well as the visionary foresight necessary to understand the importance of the suggestions before presenting them to you. For your reference, I have attached the details of my previous correspondence in PDF format, as they pertain to the nation's safety.

With warm regards,

Yours sincerely, Dr. Nanda Nandan Das, Original Thinker Chairman, People's Welfare Suggestion Forum

Dated: 15th October 2024,

Grievance Document

Current Status-Case closed

Date of Action-02/11/2024

Remarks-Your suggestions are always welcome. Should you have any other suggestions Register on MyGov App. You can Follow MyGov on Twitter/Subscribe to MyGov YouTube Channel also.

Regards, CPIO MyGov

Officer Name-Office of CEO MyGov (Office of CEO MyGov).

Contact Address-Electronics Niketan CGO Complex, N Delhi

Email Address-ceo@mygov.in

Contact Number-01124364706

CHAPTER V
PUNISHMENT FOR CHILDREN INVOLVED IN HEINOUS CRIME

Your Grievance is registered successfully.
Registration Number: PMOPG/E/2024/0150978
Dt. 07.10.2024

Respected Shri Narendra Modi, Hon'ble Prime Minister of India,

I hope this message finds you in good health and high spirits.

It has been observed that children below the age of 18, who are considered juveniles, are often sent to juvenile homes and exempted from severe punishment. I propose that individuals involved in heinous crimes should be treated the same as adult criminals, regardless of their age. The laws governing such crimes should apply uniformly to all, including juveniles who commit serious offenses.

Providing legal protection on the basis of age for such grave offenses, does not contribute to the development of responsible citizens. In fact, it may encourage 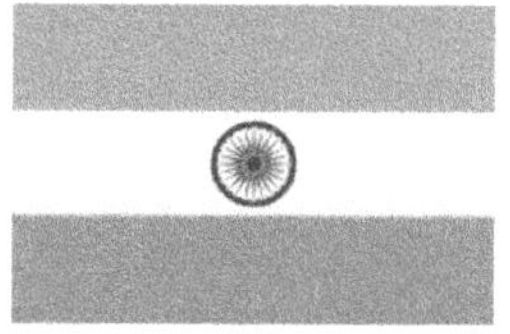 young people to commit such crimes without fear of consequences. This poses a significant threat to the moral and social fabric of our youth. The deterrent effect of strict punishment, along with the promotion of ethical values, should be integrated into our educational system.

With heartfelt regards,

Yours sincerely,   **NARENDRA MODI**

Dr. Nanda Nandan Das, Original Thinker Chairman, People's Welfare Suggestion Forum

Date: 07.10.2024   11:53pm

CHAPTER VI
THE INTENTION TO MAKE PUNJAB, SEPARATE FROM INDIA IS RISKY AND DANGEROUS FOR SIKHS COMMUNITY

Registration Number: PMOPG/E/2024/0156797

Date of Receipt-21/10/2024

Received By Ministry/Department-Prime Minister's Office
Grievance Description- Dt. 21.10,2024
THE INTENTION TO MAKE PUNJAB, SEPARATE FROM INDIA IS RISKY AND DANGEROUS FOR SIKHS COMMUNITY
Respected Shri Narendra Modi Ji, Hon'ble Prime Minister of India, The script attached herewith is submitted herewith for favour of your kind perusal. The fact is self- explanatory. With heartiest regards,
Yours sincerely
Dr. Nanda Nandan Das, Original Thinker Chairman, People's Welfare Suggestion Forum
21.10,2024
Grievance Document
Current Status-Case closed
Date of Action-02/11/2024
Remarks
Your suggestions are always welcome. Should you have any other suggestions Register on MyGov App. You can Follow MyGov on Twitter/Subscribe to MyGov YouTube Channel also. Regards, CPIO MyGov
Officer Concerns To
Officer Name-Office of CEO MyGov (Office of CEO MyGov)
Organisation name-My Gov.

CHAPTER VII

PRINCIPLE OF AKHANDA BHARAT

Your Grievance is registered successfully.
Registration Number: PMOPG/E/2024/0150147
Dt. 05.10.2024
Respected Shri Narendra Modi Ji, Hon'ble Prime Minister of India,

I hope this letter finds you in good health and high spirits. The concept of Akhand Bharat is certainly appealing and evokes a sense of pride. Some leaders express a desire to reunite the territories that once constituted Akhand Bharat. However, before initiating this idea, it is important to reflect on the cultural foundation of Akhand Bharat, which was deeply rooted in Sanatan Dharma, promoting ideals such as *Sarve Bhavantu Sukhinah* and *Vasudhaiva Kutumbakam,* meaning "may all be happy" and "the world is one family." These values aim for the peace and well-being of humanity as one.

Unfortunately, in certain Islamic countries, misguided administrative policies have led to poverty, crime, and terrorism. Peace remains elusive in these regions, and we have witnessed brutalities against Hindus and other minorities, particularly in Bangladesh, Pakistan, and Afghanistan. These acts are not only inhumane but are also expressions of extreme cruelty, which can never foster peace on Earth.

At the time of India's independence, Pakistan was created as an Islamic nation named East & West Pakistan, and in 1971, East Pakistan became a separate Islamic country named Bangladesh.

Despite this, there is not a single Hindu-majority country in the world dedicated to the protection and preservation of Hindus. Moreover, within India, certain Muslim groups contribute to unrest and destabilize the nation. The notion of restoring Akhand Bharat, therefore, could pose significant challenges to the Hindu community's existence.

Specifically, the effort to reclaim Pakistan-occupied Kashmir (PoK) may lead to an increase in the Muslim population within India, potentially creating further instability. Given our current voting system, this could enable the rise of what some call "vote jihad," which might complicate governance. For instance, when a notorious terrorist, Nasarwulha, was killed in an Israeli attack, there were open protests expressing sympathy for him in parts of Jammu and Kashmir and other regions of India.

In my view, if POK is reintegrated into India, it should be designated as a Union Territory with restricted voting rights and other necessary safeguards. Additionally, efforts should be made to establish India as a Hindu Rashtra, preserving its cultural integrity so that all Bharatiya, irrespective of religions can live in peace and harmony.

With my warmest regards,

Yours sincerely,

Dr. Nanda Nandan Das, Original Thinker

Chairman, People's Welfare Suggestion Forum

Date: 05.10.2024

NARENDRA MODI

Prime Minister of India

Name Of Complainant-NANDA NANDAN DAS
Date of Receipt-05/10/2024-**Received By Ministry/Department**
Prime Minister's Office-**Grievance Description**
Current Status-Grievance Received
Date of Action-05/10/2024
Officer Concerns To Forwarded to-Prime Minister's Office
Officer Name-Mukul Dixit, Under Secretary (Public)
Organisation name-Prime Minister's Office

CHAPTER VIII
PEACE IN BHARAT

Your Grievance is registered successfully.
Registration Number: PMOPG/E/2024/0151005

Dt. 08.10.2024

Respected Shri Narendra Modi Ji, Hon'ble PM of India.

Some political parties, in an attempt to consolidate vote banks, have sought the support of the Muslim minority while simultaneously creating divisions among Hindus by exploiting differences in religion, caste. Historically, we have seen how Jayachandra invited Mohammad Ghori to overthrow Prithiviraj Chauhan, which eventually led to the downfall and death of Prithiviraj and later Jayachandra himself. Similar actions are being taken by modern political leaders, encouraging minority groups while undermining the unity of Hindus. History has shown that those who divide their own people for short-term gains may eventually fall victim first to their own strategies.

In Bangladesh, local Islamic groups are torturing and killing Hindus and others. The atrocities committed against Hindus, Sikhs, Buddhists, and other minorities in Pakistan, Afghanistan, and other regions are well-known. These massacres are not only acts of inhumanity but also of brutal cruelty.

Respected Shri Narendra Modi Ji, Hon'ble PM, Shri Aditya Yogi Ji, CM of UP, and Shri Mohan Bhagwat Ji, Chief of RSS, have called upon Hindus across India to unite and stand strong to prevent such tragedies. However, on 07.10.2024, a leader from Hyderabad openly criticized these leaders and incited his community against them, boasting that even last one individual from Lebanon could incite stone pelting. These are only generating their community to involve in crime.

I believe that the majority of Muslims in India are good citizens who enjoy the benefits, provided by the BJP government without discrimination. However, biased preachers like the aforementioned leader in Hyderabad are spreading fabricated hatred, misleading their followers, and encouraging them to engage in criminal activities in what can only be described as "Vote Jihad."

There is not a single Hindu nation in the world. Bharat is the original home of Hindus, while Islam and Christianity are religions that migrated here. Therefore, it is crucial to preserve the heritage and culture of Hindus in India. Pakistan was created as an Islamic country to accommodate the Muslim majority, with the promise that minorities would be protected. However, minorities there have been systematically tortured and killed. This is not just inhumane but demonic brutality.

1. Promote Unity Through Peaceful Processions: Hindu preachers from across India should organize peaceful processions at the district, state, and national levels to raise awareness. These processions should follow the principles of non-violence and should not cause any disruption to traffic or daily life. Messages like "Vasudhaiva Kutumbakam" (the world is one family) and "Sarbe Bhabantu Sukhinah" (may all beings be happy) should be promoted, so that all communities, including Muslims, can live peacefully according to the values of Sanatan Dharma. Unlike Islamic countries like Pakistan and Afghanistan, where poverty, crime, and terrorism prevail, India offers equal reliefs and opportunities for all its citizens.

2. Establish Bharat as a Hindu Rashtra: All efforts should be made to declare Bharat a Hindu Rashtra, where equal rights and opportunities are provided to all Bharatiya, regardless of religion.

Additional suggestions may be added with the intention of promoting peace and unity. With regards,

Yours sincerely,

Dr. Nanda Nandan Das, Original Thinker

Chairman, People's Welfare Suggestion Forum

Dt. 08.10.2024   2:18 am

CHAPTER IX

LETTERS TO PRIME MINISTER FOR DEVELOPMENT OF ODISHA

Your Grievance is registered successfully.
Registration Number: PMOPG/E/2024/0180553

Dt. 16.12.2024
Respected Shri Narendra Modi Ji, Hon'ble Prime Minister of India
Subject: Suggestions for the Development of Odisha.
Odisha, despite being rich in natural resources such as water, minerals, forests, marine products, and renewable energy potential (solar and wind), as well as opportunities in tourism, industries, and IT, continues to struggle with poverty and underdevelopment. This stagnation crops up primarily due to a lack of visionary leadership and effective governance. However, the current Hon'ble Chief Minister of Odisha has the motive to initiate the necessary changes.

I have previously suggested various solutions to address the state's challenges to both past and present Chief Ministers of Odisha via email. Unfortunately, these suggestions have not been acted upon or given any due importance. It appears these matters have not reached the Hon'ble Chief Minister.

Therefore, I have compelled to put forth these suggestions to draw your kind attention, encouraged by your visionary leadership and the platform for direct communication that you have provided.

Below are the key issues and the registration numbers of the suggestions submitted to the PMO for your references:

1.   Poverty-Free Odisha
Registration No.: PMOPG/E/2019/0622622, dated 20.10.2019.

2.   Solution for Chit Fund Issue
Enabling the Refund of Chit Fund Money to Investors.
Registration No.: PMOPG/E/2020/0633000, dated 04.07.2020.

3.   Control of Farmer Suicides
Registration No.: PMOPG/E/2019/0614334, dated 15.10.2019.
4.   Green Odisha Initiative
Registration No.: PMOPG/E/2019/0626645, dated 23.10.2019.
5.   Compulsory Introduction of Moral Science in Education
Registration No.: PMOPG/E/2019/0640330, dated 01.11.2019.
6.   Human and Wildlife Preservation
Registration No.: PMOPG/E/2019/0621457, dated 19.10.2019.
7.   Land Reforms
Registration No.: PMOPG/E/2019/0632136, dated 27.10.2019.
8.   Control of Overdrafts
Registration No.: PMOPG/E/2019/0628895, dated 24.10.2019.
9.   Compulsory Marriage Registration
Registration No.: PMOPG/E/2019/0635673, dated 30.10.2019.
10.   Flood Management Strategies
Registration No.: PMOPG/E/2020/0800873, dated 02.09.2020.
11.   Demerits of Captive Land to Foreign Companies
Registration No.: PMOPG/E/2019/0625116, dated 22.10.2019.
12.   Addressing the Scarcity of Doctors in Government Services
Registration No.: PMOPG/E/2019/0621282, dated 19.10.2019.

The progress of Odisha depends on the actions of the concerned government authorities. A significant transformation can occur only if these authorities, including ministers and secretaries, turn Exceptional, i.e., honest, sincere, progressive, and creative. The selection of such officials should be prioritized upon their exceptional character and competence.

Gujarat's development under your leadership serves as a testament to the impact of visionary governance. Similarly, Odisha can achieve remarkable progress through innovative and focused interventions under your abled guidance.

As Odisha's governance operates as a "double engine" government, I kindly request you to forward these itemized solutions to the Hon'ble Chief Minister of Odisha or facilitate direct communication between me and the Hon'ble Chief Minister. This will enable me to provide additional innovative solutions for Odisha's critical issues. I am confident that if the above issues are sincerely dealt, there would not be unemployment problems, free of poverty, and Odisha would be a progressive state.

I firmly believe that with your encouragement and pursuit of positive steps, Odisha can become a developed state.

With heartfelt regards,

Yours sincerely,

Dr. Nanda Nandan Das, Original Thinker

Former Secretary, Works, Govt. of Odisha

Chairman, People's Welfare Suggestion Forum

Ph: 9437617604

Date: 16.12.2024

NARENDRA MODI

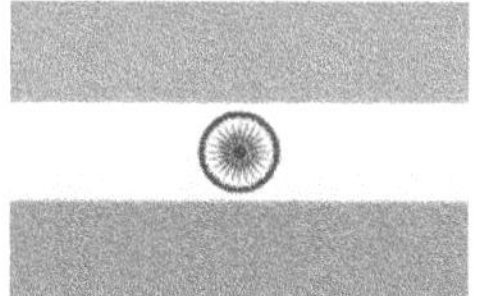

Name Of Complainant-NANDA NANDAN DAS

Date of Receipt-16/12/2024

Current Status-Under process

Date of Action-17/12/2024

Officer Concerns To

Officer Name: Sri Asit Kumar Pani (Deputy Secretary to Government)

Organization name-Odisha

Contact Address-General Administration and Public Grievance Dept., Odisha Sectt., Bhubaneswar

Email Address-gapgpublicgrievance@gmail.com

Contact Number-06742536673

CHAPTER X

CONTROL OF FARMERS' SUICIDES

Farmers often take loans for cultivation and repay them after the harvest. However, disasters such as droughts, floods, cyclones, irrigation failures, crop destruction by pests, losses from selling produce at lower prices than production costs, landslides, and even crop raids by wild animals like elephants can lead to substantial financial losses. These hardships push some farmers into severe financial crises, sometimes leading them to take extreme steps like committing suicide.

Farmers are the backbone of our economy, and their loss is not only devastating for their families but also a setback for the entire nation. However, no problem is insurmountable. The causes of these tragic incidents can be addressed through thorough research, expert consultations, and the development and implementation of effective policies.

This document identifies the root causes of farmers' suicides and offers potential solutions. If the government sincerely implements these measures and farmers adhere to certain guidelines, this crisis can be mitigated.

Proposals on this matter have been submitted to the Hon'ble Governor and Chief Minister of Odisha, as well as the Hon'ble Prime Minister of India, urging them to take decisive action to prevent further farmers' suicides.

NANDANANDAN DAS

From: nandanandan_das@yahoo.com
To: Dharmendra Pradhan, av.odisha@sansad.nic.in
Cc: Nandanandan Das
Mon, Aug 26 at 10:56 AM
This is regarding 'Control of Farmers' Suicide'. For king information Sir.

With regards,
Dr. Nanda Nandan Das, Original Thinker
Former Secretary, Works, Government of Odisha
Former Chairman, OB&CC
Chairman, People's Welfare Suggestion Forum
Ex-Chairman, Odisha Durneeti Sangharsa Mancha
Phone: 9437617604
26.08.2024
Enclosure ENCL: As mentioned above
NANDA NANDAN DAS
From: nandanandan_das@yahoo.com
To: adc.odishagovernor@gmail.com, CMO ODISHA
Cc: Nandanandan Das, Barada Prasanna Das
Mon, Aug 26 at 10:48 AM
Dt. 26.08.2024
To
The Hon'ble Governor of Odisha
The Hon'ble Chief Minister of Odisha
Subject: Control of farmers' suicide
Respected Sir,
I hope this letter finds you in good health and high spirits. The farmers' suicide has become a crucial issue in the country.
I am writing to share a suggestion submitted to the Hon'ble Prime Minister of India regarding the Control of Farmers Suicide, which has been assigned Registration Number: PMOPG/E /2019/0614334 DT. 15.10.2019. The details of this suggestion are self-explanatory and are attached for your reference and guidance.

It is requested to scrutinize through the experts and may be adopted in the state to avoid farmers' suicide.
Thank you for considering this proposal. I am confident that with your leadership, we can turn this vision into reality. With warm regards,
Yours sincerely,
Dr. Nanda Nandan Das, Original Thinker
Former Secretary, Works, Government of Odisha

Former Chairman, OB&CC
Chairman, People's Welfare Suggestion Forum
Ex-Chairman, Odisha Durneeti Sangharsa Mancha
Phone: 9437617604
26.08.2024
Enclosures: As mentioned above
CONTROL OF FARMERS' SUICIDES
Registration Number: PMOPG/E/2019/0614334
Dt. 15.10.2019The Letter No-89/odsm/2019

ODISHA DURNEETI SANGHARSA MANCHA

Regd.No.-23341/61 of 2011-12, Web: www.odsm.org.in, E-mail : odsm2011@gmail.com
489, Nageswar Tangi, Bhubaneswar - 751002

No............89..   Date.10/6/19.

Address- Pl. No-2024, CHINTAMANISWAR AREA, Bhubaneswar-751006, Odisha - PH-9437617604

Country First

To
The Hon'ble Prime Minister, India

Through Smt. Aparajita Sarangi, Hon'ble M.P, Bhubaneswar.

Sub-Control of farmers' suicide.

Respected Sir,

Odisha Durneeti Sangharsa Mancha is an apolitical organization and involves in lots of welfare of the people, basically creating corruption free activities. The experts of different disciplines are members of ODSM.

At present farmers' suicide is one burning issue in states and the country. We have formulated the process to prevent such situation. The principles to be adopted on such matter have been suggested in the enclosed paper. This may please be considered and suitable action may be taken as deemed fit.

This is for your information and kind consideration. The receipt of the letter may please be acknowledged. With kind regards,
Yours faithfully,

Dr Nanda Nandan Das   Er Bansidhar Parhi
Former Secretary, Works (Govt. Of Odisha)   Vice- Chairman, ODSM.
Chairman, Odisha Durneeti Sangharsa Mancha.
Chairman, People's Welfare Suggestion Forum

Er Jaga Bandhu Sarangi   Mr Uma Charan Mishra   Mr Sudhir Ku. Mahanti
Ex-Director, Industry   Former District Judge, Senior Advocate
Gl. Secretary, ODSM   Advisor, ODSM   Advisor

Encl:As above

dt.10.06.2019 was sent to Hon'ble Prime Minister, India through Smt. Aparajita Sarangi, Hon'ble MP, Bhubaneswar. This was on "CONTROL OF FARMERS' SUICIDES". Since we have not received any response over the matter, it is now resubmitted for favour of kind consideration.

Dr Nanda Nandan Das
Chairman, Odisha Durneeti Sangharsa Mancha
Former Secretary, Works (Govt. Of Odisha

DR. NANDA NANDAN DAS

DSc (Civil Engineering), D.Litt. (Social Works), PDF (Keisie International University, South Korea), PhD (Road), PhD (Building & Disaster), M.S.W, B.Sc. (Engg.), LLB, F.I.E, M.I.R.C, M.I.B.C

Former Secretary, Works, Govt. of Odisha.
 Former Chairman, O.B & C.C
Chairman, People's Welfare Suggestion Forum

CONTROL OF FARMERS' SUICIDE
(Nothing is impossible)

In the recent times farmers' death has become a common phenomenon in our state like some other states. Such incidents are indeed very sad. These are due to various reasons. The reasons for each case can be ascertained through in-depth study on the issue.

REASONS OF DEPRESSION IN FARMERS: -

Generally, the farmers at times incur loan for cultivation purpose and repay the same after harvesting. But when disaster like draught, flood, cyclone, failure of irrigation facility, destruction of crop by insects, loss due to disposal of products at lower price than the investment, floods, land slide and even raiding of crop by wild animals like elephants etc, results in huge loss for farmers. Thus, they are harassed and take the extreme step like committing suicide to get rid of the financial crisis.

In reality the farmers are the back bone of our economy. Their hard work feeds the country. Their death is not only a great loss to their families, but also to the entire nation. Nothing is impossible in this world. The reasons of death as cited above can be solved by in-depth study, taking experts' opinions for solutions to the problems and subsequently evolving and implementing suitable policies.

Without knowing the actual causes and getting deep into it, no policy will be successful. So, the actual cause of death is to be ascertained and based on the same the planning should follow, which will restrict the farmers' suicide. Therefore, suitable policies may be formulated to eliminate farmers' distress and consequent suicide.

REASONS OF LOSSES AND SOLUTIONS THERE ON: -

1. Losses due to disaster like draught, flood, cyclone, tidal surge, destruction of crop by insects and even destruction of crop by wild animals like elephants etc, are to be compensated by proper crop insurance. This should be compulsory for all farmers. Government is to ensure it. Government need not pay compensation on these issues, creating liability.

2. To overcome draught situation due to scanty rain, fall, government should plan the ways, such as use of underground water by lift irrigation, harvesting rain water and developing irrigation facility by constructing dams and barrages over streams and rivers. All types of water resources should be utilized to minimize the crop loss.

3. To overcome effect of flood and tidal surge, there should be flood embankment of rivers and saline embankments along sea coast and tidal rivers.

4. Destruction of crop by wild animals can be restricted by proper fencing and trench where ever necessary and insuring

crops against such losses besides prompt disbursement of compassionate grants.

5. There should be enough cold storages and weir houses to preserve and storing the grains. This will control the hike of the market rate. This is the look out of the government.

6. Loss due to disposal of product at throw away price or distress sale is a major issue in general. If a farmer spends Rs 5/- per kg of potato and sales at Rs 2/- per kg, then it will be a great unaffordable loss for one. This can be overcome by proper procurement of products from the farmer at reasonable rate. Suppose the expenditure incurred for production of potatoes is Rs 5/-per kg, then the farmer should get Rs10/-per kg of potatoes as sale proceed at one's door step. After procurement of the product the transportation cost of potatoes may be considered as Rs 2/-per kg and Re 1/-per kg may be charged towards handling/service charges and Rs 2/-per kg may be considered as profit of the retailer. Hence, the final market value of potato should be Rs 15/-per kg. This should be the look out of the government administration to ensure this. This is one example of method of procurement of any category of product and up to its final disposal. Since the farmer will get the actual profitable cost of product, he/she will never sustain loss.

In order to overcome this every village, hamlet or *pada* should have direct link with Panchayat wise Nodal officers with the assistance of local committees, who may asses the number of farmers, type of cultivations, type of crops, expenditure incurred crop wise, cost of procurement ensuring sufficient profit of farmers, transportation to market and finally marketing cost by the concerned department and also who can sort out problem of such distressed framers or counsel him/her so that no extreme step is taken. Strong vigilance should be ensured to maintain transparency during entire transaction.

7. The bankers while sanctioning loan to the farmers must ensure the purpose with actual repaying capacity. Otherwise, they will be held responsible for issuing such abnormal loan.

8. There should be provident fund deposit schemes for the farmers. These will be helpful for getting monitory saving and pension scheme.
   There are some more schemes in central government from which the farmers will also be benefited.

9. Atal Pension Yojana-Everybody can get pension of Rs 5000.00/month after the age of 60 years, provided one deposits the stipulated amount monthly in the bank between the age group 18 to 40 years. This scheme should be strictly followed by all and a targeted time schedule should be fixed by the Central govt. over states government to ensure the same and such scheme should be implemented through district administrations, so that a farmer also can get pension facility through the scheme.

10. Pradhan Mantri Jeevan Surakhya Yojana- Anybody deposits Rs 12.00 annually, if there will be death due to accident, the nominee will get Rs, 2,00,000/-. So, government should not pay compensation on these types of incidents incurring liability of the state. The implementation of such scheme should be the look out of the state governments.

11. Pradhan Mantri Jeevan Jyoti Yojana- Anybody deposits Rs 330.00 annually, if there will be death due to any cause, the nominee will get Rs, 2,00,000/-. So, government should not pay compensation on these types of incidents incurring liability of the state. The implementation of such scheme should be the look out of the governments.

12. Government may make a Fixed Deposit of Rs 4,00,000.00 against the death/ invalid of only earning member of the family, whose interest will be about Rs 2000/-per month and will act as pension for the distress families. This will be

continued till the other earning members become capable to maintain the family.

BENEFITS ON SUCH SYSTEM: -

i. The farmers will not sustain loss due to any type of disaster and less cost on disposal.

ii. The production will increase, which is beneficial to farmers and the country on the whole.

iii. Government revenue will increase and it will support employment.

iv. Finally, there will be no suicide by farmer for loss of crop. These methods will act as "AMAR LADU" for the farmers.

TO RESTRICT FARMERS INVOLVING LOAN:

Recently there have been deaths of hundreds of farmers in Odisha. Some suicidal cases are no doubt genuine, but some cases are due to some other extraneous causes. For example, one farmer had cultivated 2 acres of land on sharing basis. The yield of sharing would have been 20 quintals for 2 acres and the cost of 20 quintals would have been Rs 20,000/-. The particular farmer took a loan of Rs 2,00,000/-from different sources and committed suicide as it was impossible for him to repay the same. That means, the purpose of loan was not only for cultivation purpose, but also for some other purposes, which was beyond his capacity to repay.

CAREFULNESS TO INCUR LOAN;

13. Farmers should be very careful while incurring loan. The limitation of taking loans should be within the capacity of repayment in worst case. Government and Bank should ensure it.

14. The loan, taken by farmer for cultivation is to be repaid after harvesting, retaining sufficient profit towards one's labour. This loan amount must not be diverted for purposes other than farm inputs.

15. The loan amount should not be used for drinking and addiction towards drugs. Habit of drinking and addiction towards drugs

are not only bad for health, but also for the family and the society besides affects one's earning too.

16. At times, some farmers incur loan for cultivation purpose, but utilize it for other needs in the house, neglecting the cultivation. For such carelessness they sustain loss and thus became incapable to repay the loan.

17. Incurring Loan from banks are advisable but taking loan in monthly interest basis from money lenders is very risky, foolishness and never desirable. Such type of money lending should be banned from government side and monitored.

A proposal on land reform has been sent to Government of Odisha and has been accepted, but yet to be implemented in the policy since 2007. This proposal will definitely be a welcome suggestion for cultivators, land owners and government. The principles adopted here shall be hopefully beneficial to farmers and minimize farmers' suicides. This principle (A separate article) may be considered to restrict suicide in all over the country.

Dr Nandanandan Das,
Chairman, People's Welfare Suggestion Forum,
Dt. 15.10.2019
The Letter No-88/ODSM/2019 dt. 10.06.2019 was sent to Hon'ble Prime Minister, India through Smt. Aparijita Sarangi, Hon'ble MP, Bhubaneswar. This was on "CONTROL OF FARMERS' SUICIDES". Since we have not received any response over the matter, it is now resubmitted for favour of kind consideration.
Dr Nanda Nandan Das, Original Thinker
Chairman, Odisha Durneeti Sangharsa Mancha
Chairman, People's Welfare Suggestion Forum

CHAPTER XI

THE UNIVERSAL RELIGION HUMANITY: VISWA MANAV DHARMA

(This respects all religions)

INTRODUCTION:

THE TRUTH

The Earth got separated from the Sun in burning conditions, taking hundreds of crores of years to cool down. When the temperature of Earth became less than 100° C, water accumulated on it, then cycle of life began, leading to the present status of life on land, in water, and in the air. Human beings are part of the animal world. Due to their highly fertile brains, humans became a separate entity and exception among living beings.

People in different localities created languages, followed different religions, border lines of the countries worldwide. While the content of all religions aims at the betterment of people, their paths differ. Sometimes, these differences lead to wars between countries, acts of terrorism, and crime. Despite these differences, two common factors exist: all are human beings and belong to the same Earth, with death as a common destination.

To harmonize the character of mankind, it is necessary to adopt common principles that are beneficial and useful for everyone to live comfortably. "Religion Humanity" is the common character for all, which will make life comfortable for everyone.

TYPICAL EXAMPLE:

India is a secular country. The diverse activities of different religions can be harmful to the country. Due to personal and political interests, and the quota system in education and service, the system has become religion-based. It has even been difficult to control population growth due to religious rules. The two common factors are that all are human beings and Indians. No Indian should suffer from poverty or be involved in crime.

To build such characters, "Religion Humanity" offers a peaceful solution. If the principle of "Religion Humanity" is accepted by all religions, there will be no religious disputes, no religion will blame another, and there will be no riots among people of different religions.

Main Principles:

1. Truthfulness: Always speak the truth. If something is a secret, keep it concealed. All examples should be based on truth. Follow the path of reality. The entire universe is governed by science. This is the age of science. The development in science so far is just like a morsel of sand in the vast field of universal creation. Believe in what is scientifically true and based on reality. Any miraculous matter may exist due to causes that science has not yet reached.

2. Gentleness and Courage: Everyone should be gentle and courageous. Behaviour should be gentle. If a discussion leads to an argument, it's better to keep quiet because arguments do not lead to solutions.

3. Public Awareness and Civic Knowledge: Everyone should be aware of public awareness and preach civic knowledge. All must think that they are ideal Bharatiya and always consider "Country First." Increase earnings in a fair way and "cut the coat according to the cloth." Never be idle; rather, stay busy earning through fair means. Regular deposits in banks will gradually increase earning capacity. Health insurance should be in place for medical treatment when needed. The present insurance scheme of Rs 20.00 per annum for accidents and Rs 330.00 per annum for any type of death can be helpful for the family at the time of health care and death. The pension scheme from the age of 18 to 40 should be availed as old age financial help. Men and women should have equal rights. Both husband and wife must earn according to their capacities, ensuring they are not a burden to the country. They must also ensure their children are well-prepared to earn their livelihood, so they do not become a burden to the country.

4. Fair Judgment: Always put yourself in a judge's seat and take decisions after hearing both sides. Never interrupt when someone is speaking. Also, never allow others to interrupt when you are making a statement. Never do wrong things. Never entertain or commit injustice. Never draw conclusions based on absurd statements or arguments.

5. Avoid Dishonesty and Crime: Avoid dishonesty, crime, and intolerant activities. This will keep you away from all vice.

6. Peaceful Protests: Any sort of injustice must be strongly protested. However, ensure that protests do not lead to violence or cause damage to public or government property or life. Even in developed countries, there are ways of protesting that do not cause any loss to property or life.

7. Preplanning: Preplan all your work. Maintain a "To Do" list and follow it every day. Mark the items achieved with a tick, and carry over the rest to the next day. Maintaining a diary is essential for everyone. This way, one can accomplish much more in one's lifetime.

8. Timeliness: Complete all your assignments on time. Time never waits for anybody. There is no greatness in not paying respect to time and neglecting work or responsibilities. Make a program for any type of project and ensure its completion according to the scheduled time.

9. Proactive Approach: Never ask your boss how to accomplish an assignment. Instead, suggest your proposal to your boss and adopt the final decision to achieve successful results. This will help you improve your judgment and efficiency and assist your higher authority in arriving at a firm decision.

10. Keep in Mind:

- We have not come to this Earth suo moto.
- Some supreme power has sent us here.
- This Earth does not belong to us.
- We have come here for a few days.
- So long as we are here, let us do only good work.
- We do not carry anything when we depart from this Earth.

Hence, we should only think good and do good. Since we are here for a few days, we should not entertain discrimination based on castes, religions, or classes.

11. Respect All Religions: Never condemn or cause damage to any faith or religion. Always be eager to help others. This will prevent clashes of faith and consequently stop terrorism and violence. Let each religious person worship God in their own house and institution silently, without harming or encroaching on other religious domains. On the road and outside, all should feel like disciplined Indians. With adequate respect for the rules of other religions, society can rise to new heights; this will also erase strains among countries.

12. Problem-Solving: If a matter causes disturbance, everyone should work to find a solution. A solution formulated according to the demand of the situation will completely eradicate the problem and ensure non-recurrence. When three or more people assemble, they usually discuss the faults of an absent person or condemn politics. This is not correct. Instead, if that friend is in trouble, they should find a solution and help the friend for humanity's sake.

13. Equality: All human beings are equal and are Indians in India. Discrimination based on castes, religions, or regions and different rules according to these distinctions are unwarranted. All Indians must help each other, and no Indian should suffer from poverty or be involved in crime.

14. Idealism: Idealism on Manav Dharma, Yoga/Pranayama, and the spirit of Nationalism should be the principles to achieve good health and patriotism.

15. Types of People:
    * Positivists (Optimistic): People who bear a global vision, do things that improve society, speak and hear good things, and do not entertain negative activities. These people are rare.
    * Neutralists: People who say "let's see," "I will do it later," or believe things will happen in due course of time.
    * Non-Positives (Pessimistic): ** People who deliver good lectures and speeches, attract people through good oratory skills, quote great men like Lenin and Churchill, and events like the French Revolution & British administration, but do nothing for the development of the state/country. Many people

say that government servants and politicians have ruined everything and the condition of the country will not improve. These are non-positive people. However, there is no problem in the world that cannot be solved.

16. Religion as a Path to Enlightenment: All religions are paths to enlightenment. It is a disciplinary bondage. Religion of humanity can be inculcated into all religions through educational media. Any religion adopting this will find a harmonic environment among its people because humanity teaches humans how to be noble. A person following a particular religion can practice it in their own house and institution without affecting other religions or society. One religious person should have a friendly relationship with others, as all are basically Indians.

CONCLUSION:

This is the true Hymns (Mantra). It is meant for the betterment of the world and is the only way to achieve "Global Peace." Mass awareness is needed for its proper utilization. The "RELIGION HUMANITY" is the path to comfortable living for all without interfering with any religion. All should help each other; all developed countries should help underdeveloped countries, so that poverty and crime among humanity can be eradicated. This is the catalyst to achieve peace on Earth.

It is noticed that certain self-centred communities expand their influence by threatening and harming other communities for the sake of religion, spreading all over the world. While not all, the majority of such communities ultimately suffer from poverty, crime, and terrorism. Different divisions within these communities often end up harming and torturing each other. Such communities cannot bring peace to the Earth.

In contrast, Sanatan culture welcomes and takes care of all religions, creating a peaceful environment. Since most people do not accept the Religion Humanity, adhering to Sanatan culture can be a path to peace for individuals, communities, countries, and ultimately, for peace on Earth.

Dr. Nanda Nandan Das, Original Thinker

Former Secretary, Works, Govt. of Odisha

Chairman, People's Welfare Suggestion Forum

CHAPTER XII

ACTION AGAINST ANTI-NATIONAL ELEMENTS

Your Grievance is registered successfully.
Registration Number: PMOPG/E/2024/0162422   11:34 pm

Dt. 04.11,2024
ACTION AGAINST ANTI-NATIONAL ELEMENTS
Respected Shri Narendra Modi ji, Hon'ble Prime Minister of India,
The script, PDF format is attached herewith for favour of your kind
perusal. The fact is self- explanatory. With heartiest regards,
Yours sincerely
Dr. Nanda Nandan Das, Original Thinker
Chairman, People's Welfare Suggestion Forum
04.11.2024

 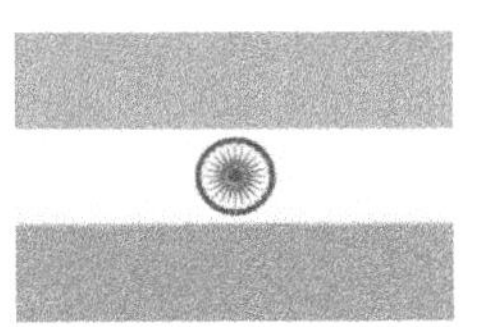

NARENDRA MODI
PRIME MINISTER

Received By Ministry/Department
Prime Minister's Office
Grievance Document
Current Status-Grievance Received
Date of Action 04/11/2024
Date: 21.10.2024
Subject: Action Against Anti-National Elements
Respected Shri Narendra Modi Ji, Hon'ble Prime Minister of
India,
I am writing to express deep concern about actions by certain
individuals and groups that seem intended to incite violence and

destabilize our nation. During the recent oath-taking ceremony in Parliament, it was reported that one MP of particular community, raised the slogan "Joy Palestine" instead of "Joy Bharat." Many perceived this act as disrespectful to our nation, and it should have been addressed at that time as an act of anti-national behaviour.

Such actions, along with the divisive ideologies they represent, should be met with appropriate legal and political consequences. This would help ensure that privileges like free speech are not misused to harm national unity.

At the time of independence, the formation of Pakistan (comprising East and West Pakistan) was intended to provide Muslims with a separate state, while India would serve as a separate nation with a deep-rooted connection to Sanatan culture. However, instead of a strict cultural divide, India has taken a generous approach, offering equal rights and opportunities to all communities. Despite this, certain groups have at times sought to impose their own cultural norms on the broader society, occasionally using violent means to press their demands.

India, as a secular nation, is distinct from Islamic countries like Pakistan and Bangladesh, which were specifically established for Muslims. Those who seek to live under separate religious laws or reject a common civil code may consider relocating to these nations or, alternatively, contribute peacefully within India's diverse society. Any demands that incite violence, promote cultural imposition, or encourage terrorism should be met with strict prohibition.

Meanwhile, Pakistan and Bangladesh, despite being Muslim-majority countries, continue to face serious challenges such as poverty, crime, and terrorism, often alongside the mistreatment of their own minority communities. This underscores the importance of fostering unity and mutual respect within India's pluralistic framework.

Bharat, as the heritage of Sanatan culture and guided by principles like Sarve Bhavantu Sukhinah (May All Be Happy) and

Vasudhaiva Kutumbakam (The World is One Family), has welcomed all communities to live peacefully. While all communities are free to practice their religion, these practices should be conducted without disturbing others. Bharat is not a religious state for any one community; thus, demands that seek to override national values with sectarian practices should not be encouraged rather denial. Individuals engaging in violent or extremist activities, like stone-pelting or harmful slogans, should face strict consequences, including restrictions on voting, free speech, and other privileges.

Kasap, a terrorist, was convicted and sentenced to death after four years, despite substantial evidence and a public expenditure of sixty crores. The case not only dragged on but also led to a significant waste of public funds. Therefore, a special court should be established to handle such serious crimes, ensuring prompt action within a limited timeframe.

It is imperative to enact stronger laws and regulations that uphold the safety, security, and unity of our country. A serious, balanced, and thoughtful approach is required to address these growing concerns.

With warm regards,

Yours sincerely,

Dr. Nanda Nandan Das, Original Thinker

Chairman, People's Welfare Suggestion Forum

Date: 21.10.2024

Members Present on the debate: Dr. Nanda Nandan Das, Er. Ambika Ballabha Swain, Sri Goutam Das, Shri Arup Chand, Shri Ananta Narayan Panda, Shri Pramod Kumar Jena and Er. Kamala Kanta Behera.

CHAPTER XIII

BAN OF CONSTRUCTION OF CONCRETE ROAD OVER EXISTING ROAD IN RURAL AREA

Your Grievance is registered successfully.
Registration Number: PMOPG/E/2024/0183917

Date: 24.12.2024, 7 AM
BAN OF CONSTRUCTION OF CONCRETE ROAD OVER EXISTING ROAD IN RURAL AREA
Respected Shri Narendra Modi Ji, Hon'ble Prime Minister
It is observed that whenever funds are available under the FD grant or any other grant in rural areas, they are often used to overlay concrete roads on existing concrete roads, regardless of whether the existing road is in good condition or damaged. This practice leads to several significant disadvantages:

1. **Raising the Height of Roads**: Repeatedly overlaying concrete on existing roads results in elevated road levels, forming high-level walls. This creates blockages in drainage systems for rainwater, causing waterlogging and flooding during rains. Such flooding disrupts the road system and affects surrounding areas.
2. **Precautionary Measures**:

o If an existing concrete road is damaged, it should first be dismantled before laying a new concrete road. This approach prevents the raising of road levels. The debris from dismantling can be used to widen roads, construct side drains, or fill nearby ditches.
o Funds should be diverted towards essential activities like drainage works, road widening, and other developmental initiatives rather than overlaying concrete on existing roads.

- o Overlaying concrete over an existing road must be strictly prohibited. This practice not only raises road height unnecessarily but also leads to a significant waste of public money. For example, overlaying concrete on a good road of a specific length costing around ₹3 lakh is an outright wastage nationally. Such funds could have been better utilized to improve the financial status BPL or for other developmental purposes.

Furthermore, it is crucial to:

- o Specify a defined lifespan for concrete roads. If a road is damaged within this period, accountability should be fixed to ensure responsible utilization of funds.
- o Implement policies to curb unnecessary road height elevation and ensure better planning and execution of infrastructure projects.

In this regard, I have already suggested these measures to the Secretary, Panchayati Raj Department, with a copy to the Hon'ble Chief Minister of Odisha. I am forwarding these suggestions for your kind information and for wider circulation to ensure effective implementation across the nation.

With warm regards,

Yours sincerely,

Nanda Nandan Das

Ex-E.I.C cum Secretary, Works Department, Government of Odisha

Date: 24.12.2024

NANDANANDAN DAS

To prsec.or@nic.in, CMO ODISHA, cc me · Mon, Dec 23 at 11:44 AM

Dt. 23.12.2024

To

The Commissioner cum Secretary, Panchayati Raj, Odisha

Sub- Ban of construction of concrete road over existing country road.

Dear Sir,

It is noticed, there is usual practice to renewal of constructing concrete road over existing concrete road. It creates not only blockage to pass the domestic rain water but also create water logging, submergence of houses of entire area, which are made grid of concrete road. Some principle can be considered for the interest of public:

If any concrete road is damaged, then the existing concrete road should be dismantled and over lay of concrete can be done. This will not obstruct to pass drainage of domestic rain water and creation of water logging in that locality. The dismantled debris can be used for widening the road and useful for drainage purpose.

The road side drains should be must for entire road network to check against water logging and flood.

There should not be overlay of concrete road, over good existing concrete road, which would be waste of public money.

It is requested consider on this matter, if require may be circulated for the greater interest of people.

With heartiest regards,

Yours sincerely

Dr. Nanda Nandan Das,

Ex-E.I.C cum Secretary, Works Govt. of Odisha.

Chairman, Peoples Welfare Suggestion Forum.

Dt. 23.12.2024

Copy forwarded to Hon'ble C M, Odisha for favour of information.

Dr. Nanda Nandan Das

Date of Receipt-24/12/2024

REVIEW ON BAN OF LAYING CONCRETE OVER CONCRETE ROAD

NARENDRA MODI,
PRIME MINISTER

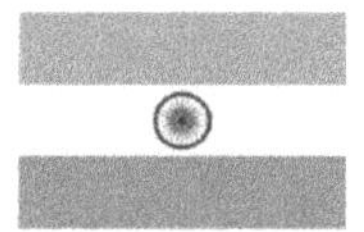

Grievance Registration Number: PMOPG/E/2025/0017776

REVIEW ON BAN OF LAYING CONCRETE OVER CONCRETE ROAD

Dt. 07.02.2025

Respected Shri Narendra Modi Ji, Hon'ble Prime Minister.
I previously submitted a topic for the "BAN OF CONSTRUCTION OF CONCRETE ROAD OVER EXISTING ROAD IN RURAL AREAS" vide registration number PMOPG/E/2024/0183917 dated 24.12.2024. The matter was disposed of with the following remark:
Current Status: Case closed
Date of Action: 25.01.2025
Remarks: It is informed that your request does not fall under the purview of MyGov. You may contact the concerned Ministry/State Government for any updates and resolution of your concerns. There is no feature on the PG portal.gov.in of MyGov to transfer your grievance/application to any Ministry/ State Government.
Officer Concerns To: Office of CEO MyGov
My concerns are as follows:
1. There is an abnormal rise in road height over subsequent years, causing waterlogging and ponding around houses during the rainy season. Solutions to overcome this issue were cited in my suggestion as per the above registration number.
2. A typical case is presented, where recently concrete has been laid over a good concrete road, which was constructed mostly a year back. The name of work as cited on the board in Odia and translated in English:
"Panchayati raj and Drinking water Dept., Odisha
Jilla Parishad, Bhadrak
Gram Panchayat, Baudpur
Name of work-Road development from Kunadas house to Mangalachhak
Project cost-Rs 1,98,000/--
Financial year-2024-2025
Fund allocation- Flood and cyclone (Dana)
Executive Engineer."
3. Over laying concrete on an existing concrete road, whether in good or damaged concrete road, must be strictly prohibited. This practice not only raises road height unnecessarily but also leads to significant waste of public money. For instance, overlaying concrete on a good road of a specific length of about 200 meters, costing around ₹1.9 lakh is outright wastage. It is about ₹10 lakhs/KM. Such funds could have been better utilized for other

developmental purposes. This issue is not limited to a particular stretch but is a usual practice nationally for the entire length of rural roads, totalling about 4,522,228 km. Thus, wastage would be abnormally high may in terms of thousands of crores and would be wastage of the exchequer nationally. This is not a state issue but concern to the nation.

There should be coordinate between different departments. So, the matter may be referred to the Finance Department to raise awareness and issue necessary instructions to concerned departments to prevent such pilferage and fix responsibility over the concerned officers.

All my write-ups are meant to raise awareness for the Hon'ble PM as per his encouragement message during 2019:

"Welcome Nandanandan, now you'll be the first to:

- Get daily updates and messages from the PM.

- Write directly to the PM - share your thoughts on any policy or issue."

Since then, I have consistently suggested result-oriented innovative thoughts and concepts on various issues. These matters were known to the authorities at the time, and while some of them might have been transferred. None of my suggestions are for personal interest but rather for the greater good of the people and the nation. I respectfully request you, esteemed Sir, to entrust such matters to a senior officer with a research mind-set, who can scrutinize the innovative, result-oriented solutions to major issues. Additionally, a special branch could be established to handle such innovative concepts on national issues.

I request you to kindly review the matter as per registration number PMOPG/E/2024/0183917 along with the present write-up. With heartiest regards,

Yours sincerely,

Dr. Nanda Nandan Das, Original Thinker

Ex-E.I.C cum Secretary, Odisha

Chairman, PWSF

07.02.2025

The members present: Nandanandan Das, Ambika Swain, Kamalakanta Behera, K.M. Mahapatra, Amiya Nanda Das, Akhoy Panda, Basanta Panigrahi, Akhoy Kumar Panda.

CHAPTER XIV
PERFORMANCE ACROSS SPHERES – FROM UNIVERSE, PLANET EARTH, COUNTRY, STATE, DISTRICT AND VILLAGE

1. UNIVERSE

- While it is known that Earth separated from the Sun, the cause behind its rotation on its axis in an anti-clockwise direction had remained unexplained. Dr. Nanda Nandan Das discovered the reasons for:

  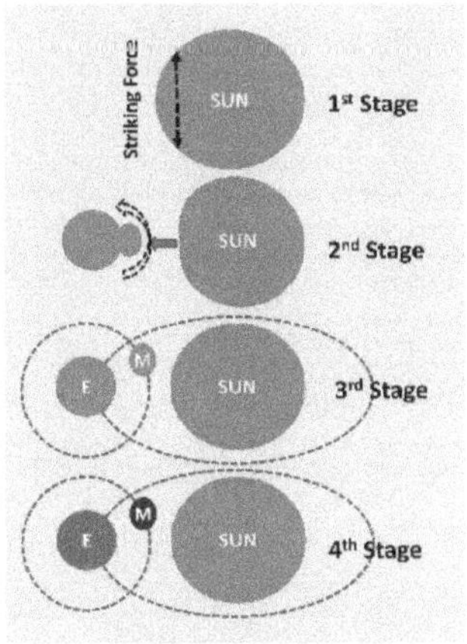

  i.   This rotation, which causes day and night,
  ii. As well as the anti-clockwise revolution of the Moon around Earth, which forms months.
  iii. Cause of magnetic field on Earth.

These findings were suggested to Hon'ble Prime Minister, India and ISRO as a ground breaking discoveries.

2. PLANET EARTH

- To promote global harmony, Dr. Das authored the book 'Global Peace' and sent it to numerous countries in November 2017. Remarkably, shortly after, the President of North Korea announced initiatives for global

peace and an end to war. The landmark meeting between the U.S. and North Korean Presidents in Singapore on June 12th 2018, followed, as did the reconciliation between North and South Korea after 40 years of enmity.

- Dr. Das was honoured with a Post-Doctoral Fellowship (PDF) from Keisie International University, South Korea, in 2016. The university praised his work as beneficial not only for Asia but for the world at large. He has presented his ideas at various international seminars through PPT presentations.

- COUNTRIES VISITED- 25-USA, CANADA, BRITAIN, BELGIUM, PARIS, GERMAN, SWITZERLAND, LUXEMBOURG, NETHERLAND, ITALY, AUSTRIA, VATICAN, DUBAI, ABU DHABI, SOUTH AFRICA, AUSTRALIA, FIJI, NEW ZEALAND, CHINA, JAPAN, THAILAND, MALAYSIA, SINGAPORE, SRI LANKA &NEPAL

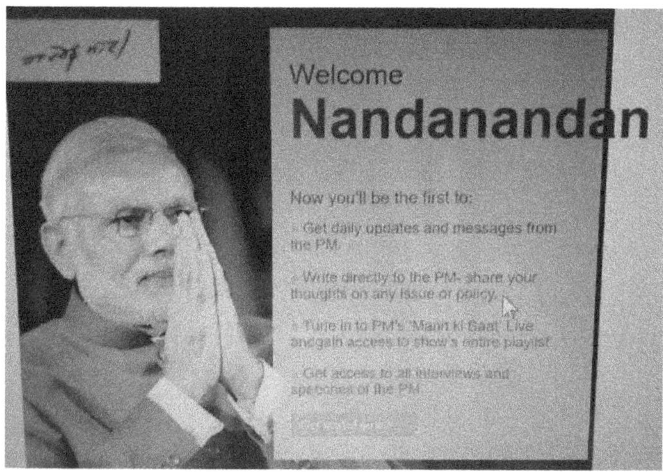

3. COUNTRY: INDIA

- Dr. Das regularly provides suggestions to the Hon'ble Prime Minister and all Chief Ministers on various issues. During 2019, Shri Narendra Modi, Hon'ble Prime Minister, India sent a message to Dr. Das- 'Welcome Nandanandan Now you'll be the first to: Get daily updates and messages from the PM. Write directly to the PM and share your thoughts on any policy and issue', Since then he is continuing to suggest to PM. His book series, Letters to the

Hon'ble Prime Minister Part 1 (IA, IB, IC) to Part X have been published and available on-line through amazon.

Shri Narendra Modi Ji, Hon'ble Prime Minister India has written personal letter to Dr. Nanda Nandan Das on 04.10.2024

प्रधान मंत्री
Prime Minister

New Delhi
आश्विन 12, शक संवत् 1946
04 October, 2024

Shri Nanda Nandan Das Ji,

Heartfelt gratitude to you for sending warm birthday wishes. I am overwhelmed to receive greetings from my family members such as yourself from across the country.

Your trust, support and cooperation are my real treasure. Your affectionate words fill me with new energy to strive in service of the nation. In the third term of our government, my resolve to fulfil the aspirations of the people and take India to great heights of progress has further strengthened.

Powered by the ability of our people and the skills of our youth, we have been setting new benchmarks in development over the last 10 years. *Amrit Kaal* is an opportunity to scale up our efforts to build a developed, inclusive and self-reliant nation.

The contribution of every Indian towards the progress of the nation is deeply valued.

With best wishes for your good health, happiness and prosperity.

Yours,

(Narendra Modi)

Shri Nanda Nandan Das
Plot- 2024, Chintamaniswar Area
Bhubaneswar, District- Khordha
Odisha- 751006

(Dr. Nanda Nandan Das's birthday greet from Shri Narendra Modi, Hon'ble Prime Minister, India.)

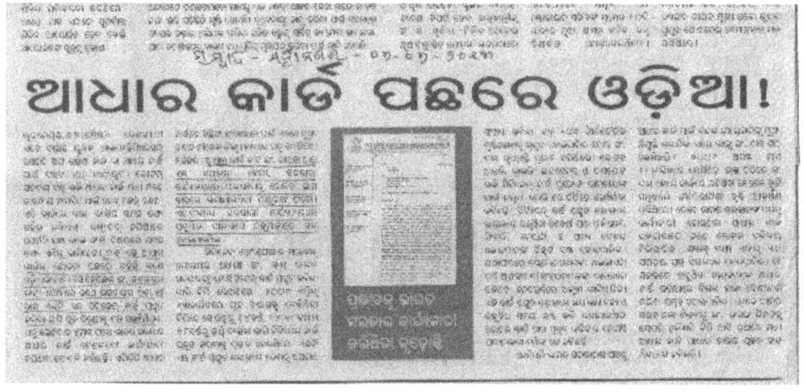

He played a role in the Aadhaar initiative through his 2009 recommendation to the Ministry of Home Affairs for an Indian Citizenship Card, a suggestion that gained media attention in paper SAMBAD as "Aadhaar Card pachhare jane Odia meaning Nanda Nandan Das".

His innovative engineering techniques have been captured in the book Fine Tuning of Road and Building Projects, supported by leading academics and marketed via Amazon and I.K. International. Such practical based engineering books on actual execution are not available.   Dr. Das's book is rare for the country.

PERFORMANCE ACROSS SPHERES

VPS/R-20.08.2018/US

20th August, 2018

The Secretary
Ministry of Home Affairs
North Block
New Delhi.

Sir,

I am enclosing herewith a representation dated 8th August, 2018 of Dr. Nanda Nandan Das, Chairman, People's Welfare Suggestion Forum, Plot No. 2024, Chintamaniswar Colony, Bhubaneshwar – 751006, Odisha, which is self explanatory, for appropriate attention.

Action taken may kindly be communicated to the petitioner under intimation to this Secretariat.

Yours faithfully

(HURBI SHAKEEL)

Encl: As Above

Copy to: Dr. Nanda Nandan Das, Chairman, People's Welfare Suggestion Forum, Plot No. 2024, Chintamaniswar Colony, Bhubaneshwar – 751006, Odisha. You are further requested to kindly contact the above mentioned addressee for further clarification on this matter.

(HURBI SHAKEEL)

(Hon'ble Vice President's action over Dr. Nanda Nandan Das's suggestion.)

Dated :

Dear Dr. Das,

I am in receipt of your letter along with a copy of the February, 2017 issue of the bi-lingual monthly Magazine 'Sahyogi'.

It is commendable that People's Welfare Suggestion Forum provides suggestions on relevant issues. I hope that the organisation would continue its activities in future as well.

With Regards,

Yours sincerely,

(Yogi Adityanath)

Dr. Nanda Nandan Das,
Chairman, People's Welfare Suggestion Forum,
Plot No. 2024, Chintamaniswar Colony,
Bhubaneswar-751006, Odisha.

(Received commendable letter from Shri Aditya Yogi, Hon'ble CM, Uttar Pradesh.)

धर्मेन्द्र प्रधान
धर्मेन्द्र प्रधान
Dharmendra Pradhan

D.O. No. 1006 ...2022...

मंत्री
शिक्षा; कौशल विकास
और उद्यमशीलता
भारत सरकार

Minister
Education; Skill Development
& Entrepreneurship
Government of India

दिनांक : 12.12.2021

आदरणीय भाई साहब,

अपने गृह राज्य ओडिशा के पूर्व सचिव, निर्माण विभाग तथा अध्यक्ष ओडिशा दुरनीति संघर्ष मोर्चा, डॉ0 नंदा नंदन दास को *पद्म श्री पुरस्कार-2022* से सम्मानित किए जाने की अनुशंसा करते हुए मुझे बड़े हर्ष का अनुभव हो रहा है। इनके लिए श्री डॉ0 नंदा नंदन दास द्वारा ऑन-लाइन नामांकन पहले ही किया गया है, जिसकी प्रतिलिपि भी मेरे इस पत्र में साथ संलग्न है।

डॉ0 दास एक कर्तव्य-निष्ठ, परिश्रमी और ईमानदार अधिकारी के साथ-साथ एक अच्छे विचारक और विभिन्न विषयों के ज्ञाता भी हैं और राष्ट्रीय व अंतर्राष्ट्रीय स्तर पर इनके परामर्श एवं सुझाव अनकों बार उपयोगी रहे हैं। इन्होंने *विश्व शांति* पर कई ग्रंथ लिखे हैं, जिनके लिए उनको अनके संस्थानों द्वारा सम्मानित किया गया है।

अत: विश्व शांति के अलावा अनेक सामाजिक समस्याओं के निराकरण में इनके उल्लेखनीय योगदान को ध्यान में रखते हुए मैं इन्हें *पद्म श्री पुरस्कार-2022* से सम्मानित करने की जोरदार अनुशंसा करता हूँ।

सादर,

आपका

/-

(धर्मेन्द्र प्रधान)

संलग्नक: यथोपरि

श्री अमित शाह
माननीय गृह मंत्री तथा सहकारिता मंत्री,
भारत सरकार,
नार्थ ब्लॉक, नई दिल्ली -110001

प्रतिलिपि सूचनार्थ

श्री नन्दा नंदन दास
प्लाट - 2024, चिंतामणिश्वर एरिया,
भुवनेश्वर (ओडिशा) - 751006

(त्रिलोचन साहु)
सह0 निजी सचिव

सबको शिक्षा, अच्छी शिक्षा   कौशल भारत—कुशल भारत

MOE - Room No. 3, 'C' Wing, 3rd Floor, Shastri Bhawan, New Delhi-110001, Phone : +91-11-23782387, Fax : +91-11-23382365
MSDE - Room No. 516, 5th Floor, Shram Shakti Bhawan, Rafi Marg, New Delhi-110001, Phone : +91-11-23465810, Fax : 011-23465825
E-mail : minister.sm@gov.in, minister-msde@gov.in

(Shri Dharmendra Pradhan Hon'ble Minister, Education has recommended Dr. Das's name for Padma Award to Shri Amit Shah Ji, Hon'ble Minister Home Affair.)

- Dr. Nanda Nandan Das's original ideas and solutions for addressing various issues were shared with Shri Narendra Modi Ji, the Hon'ble Prime Minister of India, through the official platform provided by the PM. These suggestions were subsequently presented in various forums, including field implementations, the Parliament and United Nations, on multiple occasions. The Prime Minister's Office (PMO) has taken these suggestions into consideration, and the PMO frequently seeks Dr. Das's feedback on their resolutions over the phone, requesting him to rate their performance.

- RASHTRIYA GOURAV AWARD "CERTIFICATE OF EXCELLENCE" Presented to ER NANDA NANDAN DAS for Meritorious Services, Outstanding Performance and Remarkable Role. By Dr G.V.G. KRISHNAMURTHY, HON'BLE FORMER ELECTION COMMISSIONER- DURING 2004.

4. STATE: ODISHA

- Dr. Das successfully managed major road projects like the Daitari-Paradip Expressway and Sambalpur-Rourkela State Highway 10. His new concepts in roads, buildings, and disaster management became state policies.
- As E.I.C and Secretary, he made some principles to maintain transparency in distribution of LC and circulated

to concerned departments. Thereby there were control of creation of liabilities

- Due to overdraft, Odisha suffered financial crisis and the staffs were not getting salaries regularly. His suggestion on financial policies was implemented by Shri Prafulla Ghadei, Finance Minister during 2005, which helped Odisha to eliminate its overdraft crisis in 2006 and the

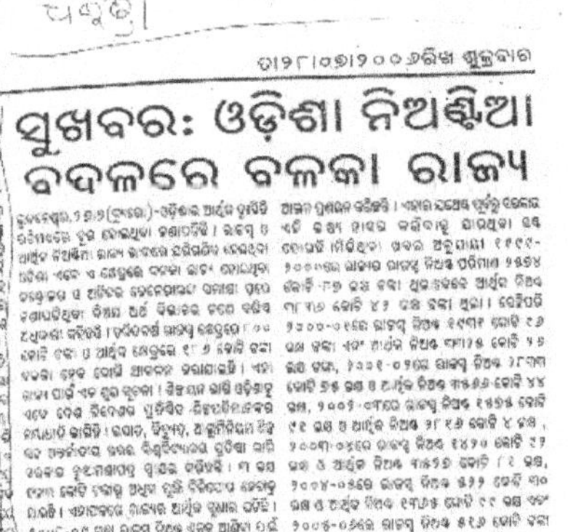

staffs get regular monthly salaries till date.

- There was an issue with people spitting on the walls in the office entryway, creating an unhygienic and dirty environment in the state. Dr. Das circulated installing idols of

Gods and Goddesses in these areas to discourage such behaviour. Once implemented, these places remained clean. Idols made of plaster of Paris were placed in his office at Nirman Saudha, and the staff began worshiping them with incense and sandalwood paste, creating a holy atmosphere in the office. This initiative was highlighted in *The Hindustan Times* in February 2002.

- As Chairman of O.B.& C.C., he reformed some policies that stabilized its financial support and ensured timely salary payments.
- He received -six times -State Awards from the Institution of Engineers, India in Bhubaneswar.
- Each year, the Dr. Nanda Nandan Das Award is presented by the Institution of Engineers, Bhubaneswar Sub-Centre, for excellence in innovative engineering.

5. DISTRICT: BHADRAK

- Dr. N. N. Das's efforts led to the construction of the new Rajghat Bridge in Bhadrak District.
- His initiatives secured Rs. 5 crores in funding, which facilitated the widening of PWD roads in 2002.
- Rs. 26 lakhs were sanctioned for improvements at B.M. Bagurai High School, with an additional Rs. 5 lakhs allocated for renovations at Bhadrak High School.

6. VILLAGE: BAUDPUR

- Dr. Das hails from Baudpur. After the 1999 Super Cyclone, he facilitated the urgent restoration of the scoured Salandi River Bridge approach, reconnecting his village.
- He spearheaded various developmental initiatives, including renovating the Pravat Club, upgrading the primary school, and converting earthen roads into metalled ones.

LIVES SAVED- (Drowning)-Rescued 4-lives from rivers: Ganges-1, Indirabati-2, and Salandi -2

He attends international seminars in various places. One example that Dr. Das as speaker in Nepal is cited here with.

Dr. Nanda Nandan Das designated as ORIGINAL THINKER

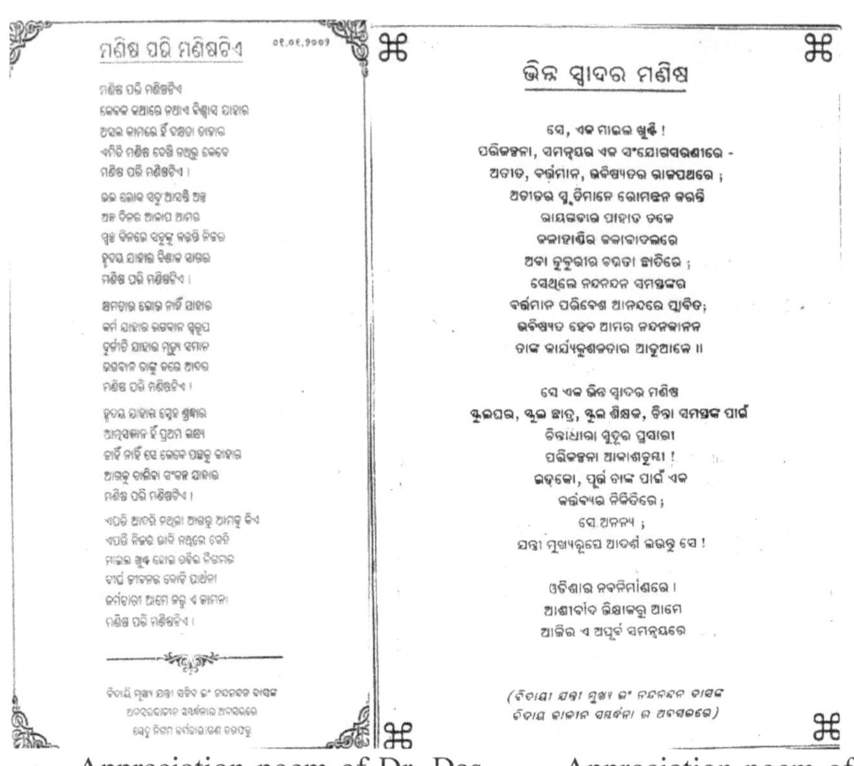

* Appreciation poem of Dr. Das
Dr. Das

from Staffs of OB &CC.
from Staffs of IDCO.

Dr. Nanda Nandan Das, Original Thinker
Former Secretary, works Govt. of Odisha
Former Chairman, OB & CC

CHAPTER XV

ENSURING STABILITY AND SECURITY IN KASHMIR

Dt. 05.11,2024   1: 02 am

Sub-Recommendations for Ensuring Stability and Security in Kashmir

Respected Shri Narendra Modi ji, Hon'ble Prime Minister of India, the script in PDF format is attached herewith for favour of your kind perusal. The fact is self- explanatory. With heartiest regards, Yours sincerely

Dr. Nanda Nandan Das, Original Thinker

Chairman, People's Welfare Suggestion Forum

05.11.2024

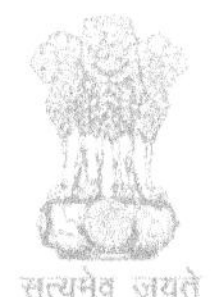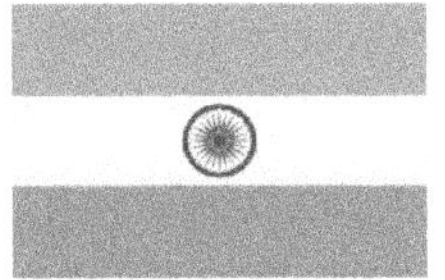

NARENDRA MODI

Prime Minister of India

Name Of Complainant-NANDA NANDAN DAS

Date of Receipt-05/11/2024

Received By Ministry/Department Prime Minister's Office

Grievance Document

Current Status-Case closed

Date of Action-16/11/2024

ENSURING STABILIY AND SECURITY IN KASHMIR

Remarks-Your suggestions are always welcome. Should you have any other suggestions Register on MyGov App. You can Follow MyGov on Twitter/Subscribe to MyGov YouTube Channel also.
Regards, CPIO MyGov
Officer Concerns To-Officer Name-Office of CEO MyGov (Office of CEO MyGov)
Dated: 03.11.2024,
Subject: Recommendations for Ensuring Stability and Security in Kashmir
Respected Shri Narendra Modi Ji, Hon'ble Prime Minister of India, I hope this message finds you in good health and high spirits. I am writing to express my concerns and suggestions regarding the recent election results in Jammu & Kashmir.

Historically, under Maharaja Hari Singh, Jammu & Kashmir initially followed the principles of a Hindu Rashtra. Later, the region merged with India, except for Pakistan-occupied Kashmir (PoK). I have already submitted a proposal regarding PoK on dated 05.10.2024).

- After independence, Jammu & Kashmir was governed under Article 370 and 35A, which granted it a special status within India. This facilitated a demographic shift, leading to a Muslim-majority region. During this period, many Kashmiri Pandits faced persecution and were forced to leave their homeland. The state experienced widespread violence, stone-pelting, and terrorist activities, leading to the deaths and suffering of security personnel, Hindus, and other religious groups. Development was stunted, and the common people lacked access to quality healthcare, education, and other essential services. Tourism, a significant source of revenue, also declined.

- With the Bharatiya Janata Party's (BJP) assumption of power, as per the government's commitment, Articles 370 and 35A were repealed. This ushered in a new era of development in Jammu & Kashmir, with improvements in communication, healthcare, education, and infrastructure comparable to the rest of India. Incidents of stone-pelting and terrorism decreased, and tourism gradually resumed, drawing people to the region once again.

- A concerning trend observed in neighbouring regions suggests that adherence to outdated societal values can exacerbate issues such as poverty, crime, and terrorism. Similar tendencies appear to be emerging within certain communities in Kashmir, as reflected in recent election outcomes. Some suggest that a phenomenon referred to as "vote-Jihad" may have influenced these results, despite various developmental achievements, economic growth, and relief measures introduced during this period. Given these dynamics, unrestricted voting in these regions could pose a security risk. Since this area needs further development for welfare of the locality, it may be prudent to consider designating areas exhibiting these tendencies as Union Territories, thereby restricting voting rights to promote stability and security.

- It is also observed that the people of Pakistan-occupied Kashmir (PoK), struggling with poverty, crime, and terrorism, have expressed a desire to merge with Jammu & Kashmir. However, some factions continue to espouse anti-secular sentiments, complicating integration efforts. Reports suggest that certain political parties, including the Jammu & Kashmir National Conference (JKNC), allegedly support these factions, inadvertently fuelling criminal and terrorist activities. This poses a significant challenge, as it could lead to a voting majority that might threaten the safety and stability of the region.

- Furthermore, recent incidents involving the targeted killings of migrant workers in construction projects within Kashmir indicate a concerning trend where local elements may aim to dominate the region by discouraging skilled professionals from outside the area. This has broader implications for the safety of those involved in development efforts.

- In light of these risks, I respectfully urge the government to adopt a strategic approach going forward. It may be advisable to temporarily halt certain development and tourism initiatives, given the potential risks of operating under an elected local government. The safety of non-native workers and tourists should be a paramount concern.

- Recent increases in terrorist incidents have resulted in the tragic loss of Indian police and military personnel, although Pakistani forces remain largely unaffected. To address this, I propose the establishment of specialized training centre's for Indian security personnel/military across Kashmir, along with the implementation of robust counter-terrorism measures. This initiative could play a crucial role in curbing terrorist activities.

- Additionally, I recommend classifying anti-national and terrorist activities into four distinct categories to facilitate efficient enforcement:

1. Direct involvement in terrorist activities.
2. Supply of ammunition and financial support to terrorists.
3. Providing logistical aid to terrorists.
4. Engagement in anti-national actions.

Individuals involved in such activities should face disqualification from accessing government services, all reliefs and be stripped of voting rights and prompt legal action should be taken to control crime.

Thank you for considering these recommendations. I remain committed to supporting all efforts aimed at securing and stabilizing the region. Warmest regards,

Yours sincerely,

Dr. Nanda Nandan Das, Original Thinker

Chairman, People's Welfare Suggestion Forum

Dated: 03.11.2024,

Members Present on the debate: Dr. Nanda Nandan Das, Er. Ambika Ballabha Swain, Sri Goutam Das, Shri Arup Chand, Shri Ananta Narayan Panda, Shri Pramod Kumar Jena and Er. Kamala Kanta Behera.

CHAPTER XVI

THREE-STORIED BUILDINGS FOR EVERY INDIAN- NO MORE POVERTY-

(Copyright of Dr. Nanda Nandan Das- Author)

Your Grievance is registered successfully.
Registration Number: PMOPG/E/2025/0005327
Dt. 12.01.2025
Respected Shri Narendra Modi Ji, Hon'ble Prime Minister of India,
The following matter is submitted for your kind knowledge and further action towards achieving THREE-STORIED BUILDING FOR EVERY CITIZEN in PDF format. These most important matters may kindly be perused, and action may be taken as deemed fit for the interest of the people and the growth of the nation.
With heartiest regards,
Yours sincerely,
Dr. Nanda Nandan Das, Original Thinker,
Former Secretary, Works Govt. of Odisha,
Chairman, People's Welfare Suggestion Forum
Dt. 12.01.2025
THREE STORIED BUILDING FOR INDIANS- NO MORE POVERTY India has been a wealthy country since ancient times, which has been the sole reason for its repeated invasions through the ages. Many foreign forces like the British, Mughals, Taimurlang, Mohammed Ghori, and even Alexander before 2000 years ago invaded the country for its wealth. Despite being invaded so many times, India is still rich. Then there should not be poverty stricken.

The methods mentioned below are not imaginary or unrealistic. If executed in a planned manner, they will yield good results.

Let's illustrate this with a story. Once there was a very poor man who always thought, "If I have gold, I will be rich." One day, while walking home, God, out of sympathy, created a heap of gold by the roadside. As the man approached the gold heap, he thought he could earn more by pretending to be a blind beggar and started acting like one. As destiny would have it, he crossed the gold heap while acting blind and remained poor all his life. Similar is the story of our state and the country. Despite having great wealth, the state is still poor and the country is developing.

For a state to be rich, it depends on its resources like minerals, irrigation, agriculture, industry, marine products, forests, and tourism and with proper 'Exceptional' governance. States like Punjab (rich in agriculture) and Goa (rich in tourism) are wealthy with only one or two of the above resources. However, despite having all these resources, Odisha is still poor. Countries like Japan and Sweden are not as naturally blessed, yet they are rich and have minimal crime rates due to their sense of morality, unity, and nationality.

All citizens and their family should be happy and not face hardship and misery due to a lack of money. A proposal containing a complete framework for a practical and realistic way of life can be achieved through the education of moral science from standard one to graduation. Such discipline and ideal citizens can be generated through moral values in the educational curriculum. This course of moral science has been suggested to the Hon'ble Prime Minister of India, with registration number: PMOPG/E/2019/0640330 during 2019. Through such moral science, morality, unity, and nationality would grow among the citizens. The quality of political leaders and administrators would be of 'Exceptional' (honest, sincere, progressive, and innovative) character, and common citizens would exhibit 'Outstanding' (honest, sincere, and progressive) nature, who would be exemplary.

The labourer or mason who is diligent and sincere will be preferred for employment and will have a regular source of income, leading to a better financial position. Similarly, if someone works honestly and hard in any private sector, they will enjoy more responsibility and a higher salary. They may even be approached by other companies with elevated perks. Therefore, if every citizen of India becomes honest, sincere, and progressive in character, they will undoubtedly have a better financial condition.

Students up to standard III will learn that despite their differences in caste, religion, and language, they are fundamentally Indians. Their only duty is to ensure that they and their surroundings are well kept. Students from 4th to 10th standards will learn that even if they live for 100 years, their days are limited, and they have come to this world for a few days as guests to do good work. They will learn how to lead a prosperous life with small earnings and own at least a three-storied building. Students should be smart and sober, undergoing NCC, Scout, Guide, and military training during vacations through the course. The following practical innovating examples for creating awareness are included in such educational curriculum.

Let us examine this arrangement with an example. Suppose a person earns Rs. 500.00 per day, should save Rs. 200.00 every day (in a bank or post office) and manage to live his day within Rs. 150.00 (the rest to be managed for no labor days) from the first day. In the process, one will save Rs. 6,000.00 per month and Rs. 72,000.00 per year. Further, the person will save about Rs. 3,75,000.00 (with interest) within five years. Following a similar process, the person can save Rs. 7,50,000 in 10 years. The person can buy a 20' x 30' plot of land near a village or the periphery of a town at a reasonable price and construct a house of size 18' x 11', including a toilet of 4' x 5' and a kitchen space of 4.5' x 5'. The house of this size on the ground floor should cost around Rs. 3.5 lakhs. Similarly, the second story will cost around Rs. 3.00 lakhs, which means a two-storied building can be constructed with Rs. 6.5 lakhs. Following a similar saving process, the person can save enough money to build a three-storied building in the subsequent years. If required, outside plastering can be avoided to save immediate expenses, and low-cost doors and windows without thresholds can be used. Concrete jali or honeycomb brickwork, concrete joineries can be used in the doors and windows as alternatives. Such construction of a house by an individual can be achieved through their own effort rather than waiting for PM Awash Yojana.

After the house is constructed, the owner can stay on the middle floor and rent out the top and ground floors. This will help them generate more wealth and provide security to their house in their absence. This process is intended for ten years. Within a further thirty years, it would be self-sufficient for a common livelihood.

Persons with higher earnings can plan proportionally. The wife should not be a housewife only. She can venture into small-time handiworks like making and selling pickles, papadum, stitching, etc. If required, the husband could opt for overtime to enhance his earnings so that the couple can lead a prosperous life till the end.

With the current demographic scenario in India, there is no need for more than one child. It is generally observed that parents face severe financial strain after having many children. The expenses of daughters' marriages and sons' education are so high that people often sell all their property for these causes and are left with nothing towards the end of their lives. The same children, instead of caring for their old parents, fight for the property and harass them. This is why a majority of India's elderly suffer today.

Every person should be aware of this from the student stage and plan their life accordingly. One should plan their life, earnings, and expenses so that neither they nor their family becomes a burden to the country. Everyone should save in such a manner that even if their children do not look after them, the couple would be financially sound enough to support themselves in old age. The investment process should be such that even if one does not work in old age, the investments provide enough dividends. Nowadays, medical treatment is more of a business than a service. Therefore, appropriate insurance should be taken at a young age to ensure good treatment and checkups in old age.

However, within one decade, the present government has taken various initiatives to raise individual incomes and take care of health status. Such advantages should be utilized.

To live a good life, one has to plan from the beginning. With all kinds of planning and hard work, it is necessary for a person to take time off on weekends, spend quality time, and enjoy with their family.

Dos and Don'ts:

1) Consumption of alcohol and other addictions should be avoided. If a person spends Rs. 100.00 daily on addictions, they would spend Rs. 3,000.00 per month, Rs. 36,000.00 in a year, and Rs. 18,00,000.00 in 50 years, which could otherwise be savings. These expenses happen unwittingly when addicted. So, all kinds of addictions should be avoided.

2) Boy or girl, have only one child. It is a pure social fallacy that only boys carry the family name forward. One should rise above these backward thoughts and be happy with whatever child they have.

3) One should not do injustice to themselves, their surroundings, or others.

4) One should not be dishonest.

5) One should consider themselves an Indian first and remember they are here for a limited number of days and should not harm anybody.
6) One should control their anger, jealousy, highhandedness, and be courteous to ladies, refraining from conspiracy and harming others.
7) One should avoid taking loans. Even if a loan must be taken, avoid loans based on monthly interest as this will ruin future life.
8) One must cut the coat according to the cloth. It means one should be limited to spend with the income.

By considering themselves as honest, adept, and cooperative Indians and planning their lives as stated above, individuals will benefit themselves and their surroundings. If every citizen practices the above, there will be no poverty in the country, and India shall become a prosperous nation.

Dr. Nanda Nandan Das, Original Thinker
Former Secretary, Works, Govt. of Odisha
Ex-Chairman, O.B & C.C
Chairman, People's Welfare Suggestion Forum
Ex-Chairman, Odisha Durneeti Sangharsa Mancha
Phone: 9437617604

CHAPTER XVII

REVISION OF CONSTITUTION

Your Grievance is registered successfully.
Registration Number: PMOPG/E/2025/0015628
Dt. 02.02.2025

Respected Shri Narendra Modi Ji, Hon'ble Prime Minister of India.

I hope this message finds you in good health and high spirits. Attached herewith is a document on the topic of 'Revision of Constitution,' which is self-explanatory. Kindly peruse and address it as deemed suitable.

I seek a clarification:

At times, suggestions are disposed of with a remark:

Current Status: Case closed.

Remarks:

"It is informed that your request does not fall under the purview of MyGov. You may contact the concerned Ministry/State Government for updates and resolution of your concerns. There is no feature on the PG portal.gov.in of My Gov to transfer your grievance/application to any Ministry/State Government."

At the age of 82, I have been suggesting ideas to the Hon'ble PM since 2019, encouraged by PM's message 'Write directly to PM and share your thoughts on any policy or issue,' which is cited in the attached file. All my thoughts are innovative and intended for the greater good of the people, the country, and global peace. Though not physically well, I remain all alone in the village of Baudpur to keep my mind free from tension and other forces, with the support of a caretaker, away from family, except occasions. Most of my thoughts are generated instantly, often in the dead of night when the atmosphere is calm.

Therefore, I request that all my suggestions be scrutinized by authorities with 'exceptional' (honest, sincere, progressive, and innovative) research mindsets to ensure proper financial status improvement, discipline, progress, and solutions to various issues. All the scripts are solution-oriented and should be referred to the concerned departments as special cases, which would certainly give contentment that the painstaking efforts aren't getting ignored. These scripts are segmented into twelve different books 'Letters to the Hon'ble Prime Minister' and available online.

With heartiest regards,

Dr. Nanda Nandan Das, Original Thinker

Former Secretary, Works Govt. Odisha

Former Chairman, OB&CC

Chairman, People's Welfare Suggestion Forum

02.02.2025

Encl: Attached file

REVISION OF CONSTITUTION

The Republic Day of India is celebrated on 26th January 1950, marking the day when the policies of the constitution became the rules to govern the country. For the welfare of the citizens, governments become responsible, and the constitution sets the rules to be followed by the governments for such purposes. When the constitution was finalized, it was made considering the then situation of India.

The condition of the people of the country was as follows: India gained independence on 15th August 1947. The people had been under the rule of the British, Mughals, and various kings for thousands of years. As a result, they were unaware of their rights. There were no facilities such as communication, health, education, electricity, water supply, sanitation, agriculture, proper housing, and they faced oppression from landlords and kings. The people were poverty-stricken.

The constitution was highly beneficial for the country, considering the future welfare of the citizens. It was truly excellent, even during the crucial time of independence, thanks to the efforts of Dr. Ambedkar and others.

REASONS FOR REVISION OF CONSTITUTION

The present status of the citizens is different:

1. There are facilities for communication, education, health, electricity, water supply, cleanliness through Swachh Bharat, opening of bank accounts with zero balance, strong defense, development of agricultural facilities, advanced railway and air transport, development of IT, UPI transactions, FASTag arrangements at toll gates, and an improved financial status of the citizens. To maintain discipline in such development, there should be proper policies in the government to bring morality, unity and feeling of nationality.

2. There are issues of crime, terrorism, and religious disputes, which often result in violence. Proper guidance is needed to control these issues.

3. There have been wars between India and Pakistan and repeated disputes with China. Proper steps should be taken to overcome such problems.

4. Pakistan gained independence one day earlier than India and was declared a Muslim country due to its Muslim majority. Similarly, India could have been declared Hindustan due to its Hindu majority.

5. Presently, it is observed that India is in a much better condition than Pakistan due to the prevalence of Hindu culture with its system of moral values and the principle of considering all as part of the same human family.

6. As per the principles of Sanatan Dharma, the sayings "Sarve Bhavantu Sukhinah" and "Vasudhaiva Kutumbakam" are meant for the peace of entire mankind, irrespective of religions, castes, or any other differences.

7. As a predominantly Muslim country, Pakistan has seen a significant reduction in the population of Hindus, Sikhs,

Christians, and other religious groups. There are also disputes among different groups within the same religion. Issues such as poverty, crime, and the encouragement of terrorism have been attributed to the country's mode of administration. Since independence, Pakistan has had a contentious relationship with India. Similarly, in Bangladesh, some Hindu and other religious communities have faced violence and persecution. These issues should be addressed to ensure the stability and safety of all religious groups.

8. A community created about 1400 years ago has spread to 57 countries of the world. Many of these countries encourage terrorism and kill natives and other religious persons to expand their religion. They subdivide the religion into different groups and create violence. However, there are exceptions in countries like Dubai, Abu Dhabi, UAE, and many more, which do not tolerate crime and terrorism and encourage other communities.

9. The war between Hamas and Israel, started by a terrorist attack by Hamas on 7th October 2023, targeted school areas, medical areas, and religious zones, which are usually not attacked even during war on humanitarian grounds. Such situations may exist in other countries as well. Under such circumstances, it would never be possible to achieve peace on Earth.

10. The war between Russia and Ukraine has been ongoing for years.

11. Some Muslims in India have openly declared their intention to make India a Muslim country by 2047 and have started threatening and continuing their mission.

12. In the past, many invaders and terrorists attacked our country. They not only killed the natives but also destroyed Hindu temples and erected their institutions over them. This narrow-mindedness and low mentality of such groups should be condemned. They could have constructed their structures without damaging Hindu temples.

13. During independence, the people were mostly illiterate, divided by caste and religion, and had a strong sense of rich-poor disparity. If, after India gained independence, moral science had

been introduced as a compulsory subject based on the principle of "Country First," and all citizens identified as Bharatiya/Indians with other differences being secondary, our country would probably have become a developed nation within two decades. Such feelings can only be generated through the inclusion of moral values in the educational curriculum. A proposal has been made to the Hon'ble Prime Minister (Registration number-PMOPG/E/2019/0640330 Dt. 01.11.2019) to include Moral Science as a compulsory subject from class 1 to graduation. Morality will grow among citizens through moral values in the educational system and two category citizens i.e. outstanding (honest, sincere, and progressive) and Exceptional outstanding (honest, sincere, progressive and creative/innovative) would be generated to push forward to make our country developed.

14. It is observed that citizens are harassed when involved in court matters. There are many pending cases in all courts. For example, Mohammed Ajmal Amir Kasab, the terrorist involved in the 26/11 2008 attack, was executed in November 2012. About 60 crores of rupees were spent on his stay for four years. This not only encourages crimes but also wastes public money and time. Heinous crimes should be dealt with as a priority, and cases should be closed within two months if the proofs are confirmed. All heinous crimes should be dealt with by special courts or defense courts to ensure prompt action. The recent attack and brutal murder of Kaneilal and similar crimes should be dealt with through special courts to provide proper justice.

15. The judicial system of our country has continued in its British form for hundreds of years. All rules should be the same for all Indians, irrespective of religion, caste, or regional differences.

16. Initially, the quota systems were permitted for ten years, but these have been availed by the creamy class people of these categories till date, violating the terms of 10 years and ignoring the right of availing quota by the actual poor (BPL) of these categories. Quotas and other facilities to raise the status of all poor, irrespective of any class, should be permitted for a certain

period, say another 10 years, so that the entire country would be free of poverty. It is felt that political parties mostly don't want to eliminate the creamy class from their concerned quota system to avoid losing their vote bank. However, such creamy persons should be debarred from getting such quotas, allowing these facilities to be availed by BPL (Below Poverty Line) categories.

17. It is noticed that the Constitution of India has been amended 106 times. Some amendments have been made to benefit particular communities and strengthen vote banks. Such matters should be taken into account.

18. All religions should be considered with equal status, and religious activities should be observed in their own houses and institutions, not openly. Any mass gatherings can be observed with a representative from the district administration.

19. The heritage of the country concerning Sanatan Dharma should always be maintained.

20. The creation of problems by insulting the speaker and vacating parliamentary/assembly sessions should be considered insulting to the house. Therefore, it should be restricted.

21. Freebies for political parties in the states should be strictly banned, as they would be a sheer wastage of public money and retard development.

22. All states should be subordinate to the central government. The reliefs needed for the welfare of citizens should be looked after by the central government, and all states should obey the instructions within a particular time-bound period.

23. In no case should parties leave parliamentary sessions; it should be banned. The leaders are people's representatives, and their leaving the hall in protest would be a misuse of public money.

24. Open public strikes causing obstruction to road and railway transportation systems should be banned. Any such protests should be communicated through the concerned public representatives, such as MLAs and MPs. These leaders would justify the public protests to the government, meaning the concerned minister with supporting government authorities of the particular department.

25. There should be strict restrictions on false promises and misleading statements made about other parties during election campaigns. Creating liabilities for the state hinders development and leads to poverty. Accountability should be established for those responsible for creating such liabilities.

26. The country has ample resources. With morality, unity, and a sense of nationality among all citizens, it would take no time to become a developed and ideal country in the world. Such morality, unity, and a sense of nationality among all citizens can be generated through moral values over time, as indicated in item 13, and strong enforcement of laws.

27. It is often noticed that there is not much direct connection between MLAs and MPs with the public during their tenure. It is suggested to entrust MLAs with state matters and MPs with national matters to ensure the development of their respective jurisdictions, in coordination with the district administration. Such an initiative would lead to rapid progress in development for the entire nation. If such an initiative had been adopted after independence, our country would probably have become a developed country much earlier.

Dr. Nanda Nandan Das, Original Thinker
Former Secretary, Works Govt. Odisha
Former Chairman, OB&CC
Chairman, People's Welfare Suggestion Forum
Dt. 02.02.2025

CHAPTER XVIII

HAPPY NEW YEAR AND BLESSING TO NEWLY WEDDED COUPLE

Your Grievance is registered successfully.
Registration Number: PMOPG/E/2025/0000003

Dt. 01.01.2025   00:03 AM

Respected Shri Narendra Modi Ji, Hon'ble Prime Minister of India,

WISH YOU A HAPPY NEW YEAR

The details of my gratitude for your letter dated 04.10.2024, addressed to me, along with the invitation and your blessings for the marriage ceremony of my grandson Nayan and Bindiya, are attached herewith for your kind information.

With heartiest regards,

Yours sincerely,

Nanda Nandan Das, Original Thinker,

Chairman, People's Welfare Suggestion Forum

01.01.2025

ATTACHED PDF

01.01.2025

Respected Shri Narendra Modi Ji, Hon'ble Prime Minister of India

WISH YOU A HAPPY NEW YEAR

May God bless you with happiness and prosperity. As we step into 2025, it marks not only a new beginning but also a renewed commitment to furthering the development of our country and achieving global peace.

I was overwhelmed to receive your personal letter dated 04.10.2024, addressing me as a family member. Your words, "Your trust, support, and cooperation are my real treasure. Your affectionate words fill me with new energy to strive in service of the nation," brought immense joy and renewed vigour to me, even at the age of 80+. I believe no one might have received such a heartfelt greeting from any previous Prime Ministers. It is undoubtedly a great lifetime award for me.

  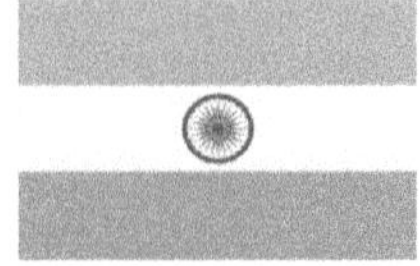

NARENDRA MODI, *Prime Minister of India*

My grandson Nayan, son of my eldest son Shri Sachi Nandan Das and Purnima Das, will marry Bindiya on 19th January 2025. The

invitation card and request to attend are enclosed herewith. Your blessings to the young couple would bring them joy and energy for their future happiness and prosperity.

With heartiest regards,

Yours sincerely,

Nanda Nandan Das, Original Thinker,

01.01.2025

Current Status-Case closed

Date of Action-02/01/2025

Reason-Others

Remarks-Sent to unit concerned

Blessings from the Prime Minister to Nayan and Bindia on Their Marriage

On 19.01.2025, Nayan (Shree nandan) and Bindiya (Priyadarshini) were happily married. The 'wedding feast' took place at the Durene Hotel in Bhubaneswar on 22.01.2025. Shree Nandan Das is the son of Purnima and Sachi Nandan, and the grandson of Dr. Nanda Nandan Das, former Works Secretary.

On the day of the wedding feast, the newlywed couple received a blessing message from Shri Narendra Modi, Prime Minister of India. Such wonderful news is being shared to seek the good wishes and blessings of everyone.

Dr. Nanda Nandan Das,

Former Works Secretary

Chairman, People's Welfare Suggestion Forum

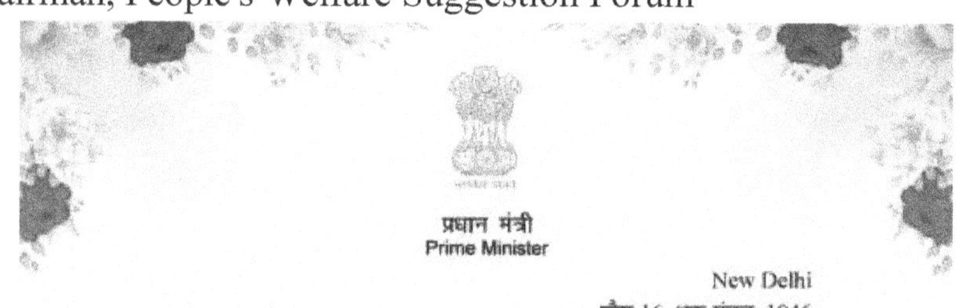

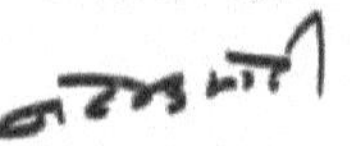

CHAPTER XIX
POINTS FOR CONSIDERATION FOR CEASEFIRE

Registration Number: PMOPG/E/2025/0065748

Dt. 10.05.2025   20:14 pm

Respected Shri Narendra Modi Ji, Hon'ble Prime Minister of Bharat

Due to the mutual understanding between the Director Generals of Military Operations (DGMO) of Pakistan and India, a ceasefire has been implemented from 5 PM today, easing the tension of war between both nations. This is undoubtedly an encouraging and positive development.

In light of this, I humbly present a few key points for consideration in the upcoming negotiations:

1. **Complete Eradication of Terrorism:** All terrorist activities must be entirely eliminated to ensure peace and security in the region.
2. **Universal Brotherhood:** Humanity transcends borders and religions. We are all part of the same global family, and differences in faith or geographical zones should never lead to misguided disputes.
3. **A Progressive Mind-set:** The citizens of Pakistan should be encouraged to embrace humanitarian values and align with modern scientific perspectives. Outdated, negative ideologies should be discouraged.
4. **Joint Efforts Against Terrorism:** Pakistan should collaborate with India and align with the vision of our Hon'ble Prime Minister to completely eradicate terrorism from the region.

5. **Interfaith Harmony:** Since religions serve as social bonds, people of all faiths should foster friendships and mutual respect, strengthening unity among all.
6. **Path to Global Peace:** These measures will lead to lasting peace, not only in the subcontinent but across the world.

I sincerely hope that these points will be considered during the final negotiations.

With heartfelt regards,

Yours sincerely,

Dr. Nanda Nandan Das, Original Thinker

Chairman, People's Welfare Suggestion Forum

Dt. 10.05.2025

Acknowledgment of Submissions to the Hon'ble Prime Minister

NB: The following message from Shri Narendra Modi Ji, Hon'ble Prime Minister, from 2019 reflects his encouragement to me for sharing my thoughts directly with him for his awareness. This write-up is intended for his acknowledgment and reference.

PM DESIRE: Welcome Nandanandan:

Now you'll be the first to:

- **Get daily updates and messages from the PM.**
- **Write directly to the PM, share your thoughts on any issue or policy.**

Inspired by this encouraging message in 2019, I have been consistently proposing original ideas and solutions to address critical societal, national, and global concerns. These recommendations have been meticulously compiled into a twelve-part book series titled *Letters to the Hon'ble Prime Minister*, which is available on various online platforms.

This body of work is intended for the awareness of the Hon'ble Prime Minister, in alignment with his vision. Kindly ensure this is acknowledged.   With heartiest regards,

Yours sincerely,

Dr. Nanda Nandan Das, Original Thinker

Chairman, People's Welfare Suggestion Forum

Dt. 10.05.2025